THE GREATEST SALES BOOK EVER WRITTEN

HOW TO BECOME A TOP SALES REPRESENTATIVE OR THE BEST AT ANYTHING YOU DO

By Dean Gould

Dean Gould
& Associates

Visit me on the website at www.deangould.com

In Loving Memory of

Lois Gene Gould

DEDICATION

I dedicate this book to my beautiful wife Alissa, best friend and partner. She puts up with my long hours and constant traveling. She guides and supports me in everything I do. She has added another dimension in my life that makes it even more worth while. Also, thanks to my mom and dad, Lois and Gerry. They provided me with love, support, compassion for others, knowledge, a strong work ethic, the difference between right and wrong, a college education, responsibility, accountability, and a great childhood. They also forced me to quit dreaming and take action.

Thanks to my sister Beth Alhanti, for her opinions through the process of writing this book. She also worked for Johnson and Johnson and became Rookie of the Year and then Sales Rep of the Year two years later. She is one who exemplifies many of the traits described in this book and I am very proud of her. Thanks to my late brother, Randy, for his guidance during the tough times. His strength and dignity were amazing. Thanks to my brother Cary, for his friendship and for teaching me about giving of oneself to help others. Also, thanks to my brother David Gould, a professional writer and marketer extraordinaire, for his advice and council. Thanks to my dad's wife, Judy, for her help, support, and suggestions for my website.

Arthur Kessler started Youth Baseball in Lehigh Acres, Fl. By some mysterious coincidence, I ended up on the Orioles, with his son Phil. The Orioles were the only team to ever go undefeated in a season, in Lehigh, and you can imagine the impact that stretch of winning had in my life. "Uncle Art" was a man's man and a great role model. His wife, "Aunt" Myra, has given me 40 plus years of sound advice and love. While I was a single sales rep on the road, after my mother passed away, Myra cooked me some of the best home cooked meals. You have to eat well when you're a hard working sales rep. She is also a professional writer who provided great ideas for the book.

I am grateful to have two great in-laws, Bob and Caryn Fagan, who support me in anything I do and also provide us with sound advice.

Jim Brunswick, a top horse trainer and coach, also taught me how to be a winner on the back of a Quarter Horse. I have carried those lessons of life throughout my years. His lessons on patience and other important virtues, while horse training, helped me in many other facets of life as well. He helped guide me and my horses to win three straight Youth Reining Championships, 1971-73.

Most importantly, thank God for all the blessings in my life; a great wife, a wonderful family, the best friends in the world, great health, success, strength to move forward, and the life experiences to write this book. What more could anyone hope for?

ACKNOWLEDGEMENTS

I want to thank the following people who have been instrumental in my success and career. They are my mentors, my managers, and people who worked for me. Without them, I could not have achieved all that I have as I was given opportunities and knowledge by each of these people along the way.

I am forever indebted to the following people. In the order in which we met: Richard Moorhead, Dave Goldin, Howard Miller, Jay Speelhoffer, Rick Puleo, Doug Elkin, Jim Webb, Debbie Goldstein, Alan LeBlanc, Charlie Lechner, Jeff Oveland, Bob Coradini, Chris Frederick, Carol Zilm, Manny Asser, Alex Martin, Paul Gotsch, Mike Mussallem, and Chris Schneider. Thank you.

This book would not be possible, had it not been for the 87 sales reps and managers who I managed. They had a strong impact on my career, hence influencing the writing of this book. They taught me a tremendous amount along the way on how to be an even better sales rep and manager. Most notably I'd like to thank the following nine reps: Bryan Abe, Ben Alfelor, Terry Bates, Bret Bruneman, Scott Finger, Mike Kriz, Chris Stergion, Robert Prenter, Rick Schroeder, Tom Worthington, and Theresa Wood. These were the "winners", the top 10%'ers, the one's that got on stage every year. They were not only the "Best of the Best," but they also made my management career fun and easy. These were the people that strived to reach the top and they achieved it consistently. It's interesting to note that out of the 83 reps I've managed, the above-mentioned eleven make up a little over 10%. My goal is to help you end up on someone's top 10% list in sales or whatever you do!

I believe that in life, you not only learn from great people and great times, but you also learn from the worst people and the worst times. I would not change anything about my life or career. It has been filled with great successes and some incredible challenges. The challenges made me better at sales, managing and everyday living. Had I not experienced every single occurrence in my life, I never could have written this book nor would I be the person I am.

Finally, thanks to four close friends, all top sales people, who were always great listeners and sounding boards, offering invaluable advice along the way: Mario Bick, Doug Elkin, Phil Kessler and Dave Perri. Mario showed me how you can work hard but always keep a positive attitude. By playing baseball and growing up with Phil, he instilled in me a competitive spirit and provided the type of life long friendship that every human deserves. Doug has not only been a great friend and mentor, but he has been a tremendous roll model as a sales rep. I call him the "The Sales Machine". They don't come any better. Dave taught me the art of instant rapport and sincere, supportive friendship. He and his family, Joe, Isabel, and Joe Jr. taught me the power of giving to others unselfishly.

TABLE OF CONTENTS

1 | INTRODUCTION: HOW CAN THIS BOOK HELP YOU?

The purpose of this book is to give you those important ingredients that will propel you to the top of the sales rankings or to the top of whatever you do. I'm not going to provide "tricky" one-liners for you to repeat verbatim in your sales presentations or in discussions with your boss. This book is more about attitude. Grasp these concepts and "live" them and you will be the best of the best, no matter what you do in life.

Whether you are a sales rep or a plumber, this book is about being the best. Everyone must sell something every day of their life. People must sell themselves in interviews, to win bids or contracts, or to sell an idea to their boss. Think about it. Almost every interaction we have with other human beings requires us to sell ideas, a cause, political views or ourselves. Many things in life you get because you ask. So why not be the best at selling whatever it is you must sell in order to accomplish whatever you must accomplish. I can't think of anyone who shouldn't know how to do a better job of selling.

If you are a computer programmer, don't you have to sell your ideas to your manager or to customers? What if you are a machinist who wants a raise? Might you not have to sell (convince) your boss as to why you deserve a raise? Maybe you aren't confident enough or assertive enough to do that, but you should be, if you are good at what you do and you want and deserve the best.

This isn't just a book for beginners or those contemplating sales. This book is for experienced, tenured reps as well. Several top reps, who read this book prior to publication, indicated it was a great review, reminding them of things which they had forgotten or they just quit doing. For those of you who are actually considering sales as a profession or you are just starting in sales, this will give you a foundation on which to build your career and your life.

How can I be so bold as to name my book "The Greatest Sales Book Ever Written"?

First reason: Having read a zillion sales books, what's unique about this book is that it focuses more on how to become a TOP sales person rather than on the mechanics of selling. Yes, I include a few tips on the mechanics that have helped me over the years but the majority of the book is more about attitude and behavior. You see, the greatest sales reps throughout history and today possess certain traits on which I focus. They have a special winning attitude and behavioral traits that if you don't develop them you'll always be average or below average.

Second reason: I wish someone had handed me this book when I first got started, not just in sales, but when I was a teenager. It would have helped me avoid the setbacks common to many. It would have shortened the time it took me to become successful in business, sales and life. It would have allowed me to get what I wanted sooner, and not just monetarily. If you want to be successful at whatever you do in life, this book will help. Adopt these behaviors and you will be well on your way to the top.

Third reason: If you are just going into sales, how could you NOT read a book claiming to be the greatest of all time?

For those of you that are already at the top of your game, looking for one "gem" to help you sell more, much of this book will be a great review. But for those of you struggling, some of the things I say may be a little uncomfortable. You may know you should do them, but you'll have to decide if it's your goal to be at the top.

The top reps will read the book from cover to cover in a day. Average reps may never finish it. It seems average reps always pooh-pooh sales books or self-improvement books. Come on. I challenge you. Invest a few hours in yourself. It's worth it and it goes back to the saying, "The best reps do those things average reps don't want to do." Don't be average, read the entire book.

I am confident that the lessons in this book apply to all types of sales, sales people and industries. It doesn't matter if you are a horse trader, a cinder block salesman, or a real estate agent. Apply the concepts of this book and you will shoot to the top of the sales rankings, regardless of your industry. The average sales rep will say, "That has nothing to do with the type of sales in which I'm involved. I'm not finishing this book or listening to this guy." Whereas the great salesperson will say, "Let me read this book and try to pick up a few "tidbits" that will allow me to sell more. If I pick up just one idea that allows me to grow my business by 3%, 4%, or 5%, then it was worth the time."

Let me also say this. There is no perfect industry or job in this world. I have sold homes, leased office space, and sold loans. Until I was 29, I was looking for the perfect thing to sell. Don't read this book and think that the medical industry is a glamorous "perfect" job. It provided me with a great career and it is exciting. But it isn't easy, and I know I would have been equally as happy in many other industries as well. If you like people and you like sales, then put your nose to the grindstone and create success, whatever you sell. The grass always seems greener on the other side of the fence. Every industry has its pluses and minuses. Don't chase the perfect job or industry. I see so many people bounce around from job to job, industry to industry, which just delays their success. Read this book and allow it to help you be a better sales rep or employee in your industry.

At the same time, it is important to like what you are doing. You will never become successful at something you don't enjoy. You should be very careful in thinking that one industry has better products to sell than another. You should be very careful chasing perfection in products.

Finally, I think it is important to mention that as of January 1st, 2004, ADVAMED (Advanced Medical Technology Association) has officially enacted a voluntary set of codes for ethical interactions with Health Care professionals. Drafted in conjunction with the Dept. of Health and Human Services Inspector General, the codes are designed to promote ethical and legal interactions between the medical device industry and health care professionals.

I believe that most medical professionals avoid the temptation to be swayed by gifts and entertainment. Unfortunately, like anything in this world there are those who abuse their power and commit unethical acts.

There are a few examples, in this book, which discuss entertainment or ideas to help build relationships with your customers. Depending on your industry and your company policies, always stay within the boundaries of what is considered moral and ethical. If entertaining is considered unethical in your industry, don't do it. It's one thing to take a customer to lunch or dinner, to allow for quality time to discuss your products, but it's another thing to take them to the most expensive restaurant in the city, buy a $300 bottle of wine, merely to "buy" the business.

2 | HAVE PASSION, A BURNING DESIRE, AND BE OBSESSED WITH SUCCESS!

"The difference between a successful person and others is not a lack of strength, not a lack of knowledge, but rather in a lack of will."

VINCENT T. LOMBARDI

"Wanting something is not enough. You must hunger for it. Your motivation must be absolutely compelling in order to overcome the obstacles that will invariably come your way."

LES BROWN, MOTIVATIONAL SPEAKER

Having managed over 80 reps and observed hundreds more, I am certain that the most prominent trait that separates the Top 10% from the average is that they have a burning desire to be the best, and they are passionate in what they do. They are obsessed people on a mission to be the best. They strive to get things done today, not tomorrow. They live by the saying, "Don't put off until tomorrow what you can get done today". They are also obsessed with getting to the next step of the sale and they are constantly thinking and brainstorming on ways to get there. They work towards asking customers to commit to the next step of the sales process. If that means evaluating their product, they ask the customer to set a date to begin the evaluation. If it means having a meeting with the CFO of the company, they ask the customer to call at that moment and set the meeting with the CFO. No matter what you do in life, if you want to achieve your goals or be the best at what you do, you must have a burning desire.

Sure, there will always be a rep, here and there, who makes it into the Top 10% by having one good year, based on windfalls in their territory, a flawed or lop sided ranking formula, or any other "flash in the pan" stroke-of-luck. The truly great reps, however, are not "one shot wonders". They are obsessed with being the best and they do it year after year. Many people get into sales so that they can earn a higher income than they could at a desk job. Ninety-percent of top sales people are motivated by two things: commissions and/or recognition. I find that both of these things motivate most reps. So, if you are in sales and you're not motivated by at least one of these two things, you're in the wrong occupation.

I have said it time and time again: When hiring sales reps, I look for someone who has a proven track record of success as a top sales rep in whatever industry and who still possesses that burning desire to succeed. My first choice would be that they have the specific knowledge, technology base, or experience I am looking for, coupled with that desire and track record. But sometimes you can't always find that person that has all those traits. I just don't like settling for average reps period. So, if I can't find a top rep with the particular experience or knowledge for which I am looking, I'll go to the top rep of the closest industry to mine, before I hire the average rep from my industry.

The reason? Within a very short time, the passionate, obsessed high achiever will be up to a level of clinical or technical knowledge that combined with their burning desire will allow them to "blow" past the sales performance of the average achiever. You now have a sales professional that will succeed and be at the top year after year, versus the average person who will fall short of their sales forecast every time.

As I said, average sales reps may have something happen in their territory once that allows them to excel one year, but they can't ever seem to sustain it. On the other hand, top sales reps may have one year that is off, but they'll rebound and be back on top the next.

Sure, you can motivate an average rep to perform at a higher level for one year but if their attitude is average, they'll slip right back into their old ways. I've been fortunate to have succeeded in inspiring a few average reps, during my management career, to actually change their outlook into becoming "full-time" winners. But I'll be the first to admit that it "aint" easy and it doesn't happen that often. In the meantime, I'm hoping these words inspire those of you, who are reading with an open mind and an open heart, to develop that burning desire to become the best. So much more comes to you, when you aspire to be the best at whatever you do, than it will when you are happy with average. Find me an average rep, and usually you'll find me someone who always says that the top reps "got a break"; the manager likes them better; "they have more opportunity in their territory". It's endless.

I understand, that sometimes, with more advanced sales positions you will need specific knowledge, experience or technical ability and there's no way around it, but that is more the exception than the norm. I have yet to find that situation in the medical industry. Unless it is impossible to train someone in the field – and there are very few jobs where that is the case – let me say it again, I will choose passion and desire over experience every time. In several management jobs, I've been told, early on, that I needed to hire reps with certain sales knowledge or experience for a specific job. I just smile, and go about hiring those reps with the right attitude, versus a certain type of experience, and I prove the point every time. Yes, it might take them an extra month or two to catch on, but in the long run I'll have a rep that consistently performs at the top rather than always falling in the middle. If the person with passion and experience is available, I'll hire them, but only if they have proven they are the still the best and they still have the passion.

I was determined to make myself extremely successful and Dave Goldin saw that burning desire and gave me a chance. He looked into my heart and knew that I would in fact be a success. He knew that I had that "fire in the belly". That is something very difficult to fake in an interview. When you possess that burning desire, you can see it immediately in others.

A burning desire also gives you confidence, and it helps you to overcome fear. Many people enter sales with a fear of rejection and even a fear of talking to their more difficult customers. If you want to succeed in sales, you're going to have to overcome these fears. It's amazing when you finally realize that many of the things you feared weren't that bad after all.

In closing this chapter, I cannot say it enough: DESIRE AND PASSION ARE MORE IMPORTANT TRAITS TO A SALES PERSON THAN KNOWLEDGE AND EXPERIENCE

3 HAVE WRITTEN, SPECIFIC GOALS AND TARGETS

"The will to win is important, but the will to prepare is vital."
THE GREAT FOOTBALL COACH, JOE PATERNO

"The world makes way for a man who knows where he is going."
RALPH WALDO EMERSON

"The life that conquers is the life that moves with a steady resolution and persistence toward a predetermined goal. Those who succeed are those who have thoroughly learned the immense importance of a plan in life, and the tragic brevity of time."
W.J. DAVISON

Most of the chapters of this book are brief, maybe five to ten pages. This by far is the longest chapter, but by far one of the most important. In the most powerful self-help/motivation book I have ever read, Think and Grow Rich by Napoleon Hill he discovered that some of the most successful people of Mr. Hill's time all had one thing in common. They all had written, specific goals and backed them by a burning desire and passion to succeed. This concept transformed me from being an average, good sales rep, during my first year in medical sales, to becoming a top sales rep, performing in the top 10% year after year. In addition, it helped me to go from being totally broke in November 1990, to having accumulated a very nice nest egg within a few years. I believe I owe a large part of my success to that book and I highly recommend that you read it.

When I finally got the job with Johnson and Johnson, I told myself three things: 1) I would never be broke again 2) I was going to become a top sales rep within the company and 3) I was going to accumulate a substantial amount of savings by the time I was 40- years old. I accomplished all three.

I became a man obsessed with these three goals; especially becoming a top sales rep. I was a man on a mission and I would not be stopped. My friends thought I was losing my mind. Some people at Johnson and Johnson Medical, where I began my career, called me the "hardest working man" in the company. I was working seven days a week from 6am to 2am on a regular basis. Sometimes I would pull "all-nighters" until I finished my paper work and preparation for the week. I just could never, would never, be broke again.

If you write down your written specific goals and become obsessed with achieving them, this process will also help you to overcome your fears of rejection. The more you do it, the more you realize that customers are human beings just like you. You will come to understand that most customers are actually nice people, and you will eventually become personal friends with them. Sure, 5% of customers can be "jerks", but if you realize and accept this, you can get on with your mission to be successful, and learn to enjoy the other 95% that are nice.

So let me ask you, why do you want to be in sales or why did you get into sales? Again, most TOP sales people are in sales for one or two main reasons: 1) they want to earn a great living and/or 2) they thrive on recognition. If you went into sales because you like people, you want to help people, you hate being on the clock, you don't like someone watching over your shoulder eight hours a day, or you want a company car; those are fine ancillary or secondary reasons. But if you want to be a TOP salesperson, you need to adopt #1 and #2 as your main drivers.

Yes, it is OK if you like sales because you like people and you don't want a desk job. But the fact is that companies need to grow each year. They need to provide a return to their stockholders and they need to be able to provide new, innovative products to their customers. If your number one goal isn't to earn more commission, drive more sales, and/or get recognition, you will remain average and your goals won't be aligned with your company's goals; which is profitable growth.

Earning higher commissions and selling more products can also lead to wealth over time, which isn't a bad thing either. Getting rich may not be one of your goals in life. Wealth is but one measure of success. In fact, in your list of priorities, hopefully it isn't ranked above 1) God 2) your family 3) or your friends. Maybe you are one who likes to live for "now" and buy expensive toys; enjoying them today rather than tomorrow. Maybe accumulating wealth isn't your "bag". Maybe you just want to spend, spend, spend.

Some of you may want to earn as much money as possible to be able to give your children everything they need or want, such as sending them to the finest schools. Others may want to retire at age 50. Maybe you want to spend as much time with your family, and watch your children grow up. These goals are all different but they all have one thing in common: they require that "green paper". Unfortunately, many of the goals we may set for ourselves require money. Certainly, being a good parent or being respected in the community does not require anything but a good heart. I realize that these are the important things in life; but most other things in life do require money.

So, as a sales rep, set your goals to be the best, to be a top commission earner and strive to sell the most. If that's not your goal, it will be your manager's goal for you. Most top sales managers are not thrilled with average or below average sales performance. The great managers will be working to coach, motivate and move you up from being an average sales rep. Eventually, when it becomes apparent that you are satisfied being below average, they will work to move you out of the company. You should not be surprised if you find yourself in this situation if you have not been doing the things necessary to win.

Now, if your company is in a slump, with no new products, or your products have been surpassed by the competition, then to be above average may mean losing less business than the other reps in your company. You should compare yourself to what other reps are doing across the country, as that will be how your company compares you.

Many of the 300 or so people that I've interviewed in my career have claimed to be the best or promised to be the best if I hired them. I have been fortunate in having hired some great sales reps who have gone on to win many awards for their sales performance. When interviewing, I can sense insincerity when candidates say they want to be the

#1 sales rep and they really don't.

In most interviews I ask the candidates, "You indicate that you are a top rep with your current company. What do you think separates the top reps from the average reps?" With all the people I have interviewed, very few knew the answer I was looking for. Sometimes people know the answer but you can tell that they don't actually possess the qualities. Good interviewers can sense it and they know when someone is not being truthful. Reading this book and implementing its concepts will make you a top sales rep and then with sincerity, you will be able to answer this type of question. Don't think you can read this book and then fake what is really in your heart.

If I could only bottle the energy and passion of Rick Schroeder, one of the Top 10% Best I listed in the acknowledgments, I'd become a billionaire fast. This guy, from San Diego, is on fire. If you are around him for just five minutes, you'll be so pumped up and ready to go, you will break down any wall that stands in your way. Defeat isn't part of Rick's vocabulary, and he is constantly looking at different angles to attack the competition. Every year, he combines his passion with the goals of being Sales Rep of the Year and making the most money he possible can. He is ranked at the top of the sales force every year and he does end up maximizing the compensation to an incredible degree. In 2003, he told me that he set his written goals to be the #1 Rep in the Nation and to earn more money than he ever had. He called me early in 2004 and told me achieved both. Call it coincidence? I don't think so.

Yale University did a study of the graduating class of 1953. They found that only three percent had written specific goals for their future life after graduation. In 1973 they found that this three percent, who had written, specific goals for their careers and lives, accumulated more net worth than the entire other 97 percent combined. Read this powerful paragraph again. It always amazes me how people hear a statement like this, and fail to take a few minutes to set goals in their life.

This is not the first book that will point this out. Almost every sales or self-improvement book will tell you to have written, specific goals. Yet I would be willing to bet that no matter what organization you polled, no matter how many times you emphasize the importance of this concept, still only three percent of your sample group would voluntarily formulate a written plan of attack for their life and career. Humans are funny creatures.

Now, there are a few, rare individuals who may become successful without taking this step. But those people will never reach their full potential. You'll never be successful in the long term working by the seat of your pants. By just taking this one simple step of writing specific goals, you can double or triple your effectiveness.

Goals can take many forms. They can be in the form of a business plan. They can be a daily target list. They can be written on a flip chart or as input into your hand-held organizer. The key is that they must be written. After you write these goals, you must focus on them daily and back them with a burning passion and desire. Next to having a burning desire, having written, specific goals, is the most important thing you can do to become a top salesman.

A friend of mine, and former sales rep that worked for me, told me that when he began his career in 1994, he wrote on a piece of paper that he and his wife would be millionaires by the time he was 34 years old, which was about nine years away. He called to tell me that he hit his goal a few days before his 33rd birthday and within a few months later, he expected to have $2,000,000; all within 10 years. When he and his wife first set those goals, he said that he never thought it would be possible, but as time went on, and as their belief became stronger, it happened. He is convinced that it is because they wrote those goals down on paper.

ARE YOU HEARING THIS POINT? Have you gotten it yet? "Stop the tape." If at this point you haven't written down your goals, you need to do so NOW!!!!!!!!!!!!!!!!!!!

As a manager, the first thing I require, of a struggling sales rep, is that they write a list of goals and targets. It is my belief that had they lived by the "law" of having written, specific goals, and of course backed them with a burning desire, they normally would not have found themselves in a bad predicament in the first place. It's always the most successful reps who seem to know and understand this. Show me a successful sales rep and nine out of ten times, he or she will have a written

Carry goal of being hired and attus to job interview

set of goals and they review them often if not daily.

Writing down goals can also have benefits in your personal lives as well. It can help you be a better parent, it can help you meet the person of your dreams, or it can help your golf game. By the way, you need to carry your goals with you somewhere; either in your daily planner, your wallet, your purse or on your forehead. They do you no good back in your office. During interviews, candidates will tell me, "I am a very goal oriented person." Good. And I'll respond, "What are those goals? Do you have them with you?" Nine out of ten times they do not.

One year I hired a sales rep, who promised me, during our interview, he would have an immediate impact in his territory. He came highly recommended with a strong track record. His background was capital sales but I was hiring for a job selling disposable products. At the same time, I had hired another highly charged rep, hell bent on becoming the Number One rep in the country. Both reps started with rankings at the bottom of a sales force of 96 total people.

After a few months, the highly charged, goal-oriented rep, started heading up the rankings, closing big chunks of business. The other rep struggled and was working "by the seat of his pants" with no goals and no direction. For the first few months, his territory was sliding, as was his ranking. I asked him to show me his target and goal list but he didn't have one. I asked him to prepare one and to send me a copy of it immediately. I did not get the list, so I rearranged my schedule and went out to work with him again.

During my second visit I asked, "I'd like to see your target and goal list". He replied, "I don't need written goals. I keep them in my head. I know exactly what my goals and targets are." I again instructed him to develop a written list of goals and targets and get them to me immediately.

The next week, once again, he had no list. Now I was at the end of my rope. "Here you are struggling and I've asked you to do one simple thing, and you refuse to do it". I informed him that should his performance continue to slide, he would be put on a work performance program. His response was, "Are you threatening me?" My response was, "No, I'm not threatening you. I am telling you the facts. If your performance doesn't improve, you will be on a work program and you could end up losing your job."

We finally ended our discussion and he agreed to give me a target and goal list. After completing his target list, he began focusing on it, and his rankings began to climb. As the year progressed, he continued to have success after success. He began to trust me and we actually started having a lot of fun working together.

At the National Sales Meeting that year, when they announced the top sales reps, who would win trips to Hawaii, low and behold, this once struggling rep's name was called. I have probably never been bear hugged that hard by anyone in my life. I thought he might have broken one of my ribs. He was incredibly excited about his success and so was I. It is these type moments which make being a sales manager worthwhile. I'm proud to say that not only are we still friends, but he is now the Western Director of Sales for another company.

One of my favorite true stories is that of Thomas Edison. At some point in his life, he committed in writing, the goals to 1) develop a major invention every six months and 2) develop a minor invention every ten days. By the time he died, he had U.S. patents on 1,093 inventions and foreign patents on over 2,000 inventions. Had he not set this sort of a stretch goal for himself, he would have never gotten close to his incredible accomplishments; and he knew it. This translates directly to sales. A salesman without written goals is a poor salesman or one that will never reach their potential.

Now keep in mind, the concept of having written, specific goals and targets is not something I invented. It's been around and utilized by top sales reps and the most successful people for generations.

Written goals also prevent people from wasting time and prevent procrastination. You should have an objective for every sales call. Without an objective, you will spend too much time talking about fantasy football, the latest sales at the mall, or some other time waster. Without written objectives for each sales call, you will be having so much fun talking to your friendly customers, your mind will justify why you should keep "babbling on" about nothing. If you waste too much of your customer's time, they may not want to see you again.

Customers appreciate the fact that you have an objective. They know that the title on your business card says "Sales Representative". They know you are there to sell them something. If they don't want to be sold something or to see a presentation about your products, they won't see you. Don't think that I'm saying there shouldn't be any small talk. You need to care about your customers as people and not walk into their office with "dollar signs" in your eyes. I'm merely saying that written, specific goals will keep you from going to that point of diminishing returns.

I look at each year, consisting of 12 months, like a football season with 12 games. No great coach ever focuses his team on winning the state championship day after day, week after week. Sure, it may be the ultimate goal, but once they set that goal, they break down the season, week after week, game after game and set the goals and steps necessary to win each game. That is my motto; "One month at a time", just like a good coach focuses their team on one game at a time.

You must be obsessed with hitting your monthly goals. You must take the attitude that you cannot loose one game. You must do whatever you can, ethically, to hit your number each month. To take it one step further, you should then break the month down into weeks, then into days, and then into sales calls when setting goals. Whatever you are selling, you should know at the beginning of each month, how much product you must sell to not only hit your forecast and your commission goals, but to far surpass those targets. Set a stretch goal because just hitting forecast won't make you Sales Rep of the Year or earn the most commission ever.

For instance, if you must sell 250 stents, 250 valves, pacemakers, desks, cars, or whatever it is you sell, in a year, it means you must sell approximately 21 per month. So, I like to take it one step further. If my forecast is to sell 250 to hit plan, I determine what I think I must sell to be Sales Rep of the Year. How many valves did the Sales Rep of the Year sell last year? 300? How is the Sales Rep of the Year award determined this year? How is the comp plan structured? When does the big money kick in? These are the questions the great sales reps have answered by the day after the new comp plan has been published. If there is a question about the comp plan and their manager doesn't have the answer, they call him/her every week until they get the answer.

To be a great sales rep, you should set your goals much higher than to just "hit" forecast, plan or quota. To simply hit your plan means you will be average. So if your forecast goal is 250 widgets, set a goal for 300, 400, or even to double it. If you set your goal for 500 units and you only come in at 400, no one will feel sorry for you. You'll make so much money, win so many awards and get so much recognition by selling 400 it will make your head spin. Remember, focus on the goal and your sub-conscious will give you the ideas to get there.

So, if you set your goal for 500, that means you need to sell 42 per month, or about 11 per week. That means you must sell about two per day to hit your goal. Sounds a lot more manageable in those terms, doesn't it? Looking at 500 for the year, many might say, "You're crazy; I'll never sell that many". But two valves, stents or widgets per day, sounds a lot more feasible, doesn't it? Then you must ask yourself, how can I sell two widgets per day? Maybe your territory is already selling an average of .5 per day, or even one per day. Thus, you only have to sell an additional 1 – 1.5 units. That could mean you just need to get your current customers to use one more per day.

Maybe you just need to go find one more customer to use your product, giving you that one additional unit per day. It may be possible, if you currently have 50% of the business, to offer the customer just the slightest discount if they will give you 70% of their business. You can then pick up that additional 1 – 1.5 widgets per day. There are all sorts of ways to "skin a cat" but if you don't focus on very specific goals, the ideas will never come to you. By year-end, instead of being over fore-cast, you'll be 70% of forecast and looking for another job.

Another person who worked for me was falling short of forecast by about 35%. Every day he was out getting doors slammed in his face, trying to get people to use his product. He had no goals, targets or focus for that matter. It seemed to him that the territory was hopeless. When we sat down and brought things back into focus, a light seemed to go on. Rather than focusing on an annual number, or focusing on how much that area of the country "loves" the competition, we focused on the 11 widgets he needed to surpass forecast each month. This rep had been spending months going around talking to customers, shaking hands, and basically wasting time rather than focusing on the things that made him successful in the past.

We reviewed his resume and I reminded him of his successful past. I also broke things down and explained that he should figure out whatever way that he could to get into surgery. If he could get into three cases per day, five days a week, he'd be in 60 cases per month. Even if he only ended up in 40 cases per month, if they would just pull three of his products per week, he would surpass his forecast. Well, he did it and his sales skyrocketed.

HAVE A GOAL FOR EACH SALES CALL

Not only should you set overall goals but they should also be broken down far enough so that you actually have goals for each sales call. Many reps seem to drive around all day, bringing in donuts, and shaking a lot of hands with no goal for each sales call. This is what is called, "flying by the seat of your pants" as I described earlier. Having a sales call goal is the lowest level of goal setting and deserves an in-depth discussion.

Before each sales call, you should have on your target list, and placed firmly in your mind, an outcome of each sales call. Certainly, the goal of each call would be to sell something but depending on the type of products you represent, that may not be possible. What is possible is to move the sales process one step further to closing the sale. Maybe you want an "end-user" to make a call to the buyer to explain the need for your product. Maybe you want the Material Coordinator to provide you with data so that you can finalize your "usage" based proposal. Regardless as to what it is, you must have a goal for each call. In fact, many reps think in terms of the next step THEY, the sales rep, must take to further or close a sale. Another way to think about the process is to pre-determine the step you need the CUSTOMER to take in order to further the process along.

It is my feeling that less than 1% of the sales reps in this world can truly reach the top by "flying by the seat of their pants". Sure, it may happen one isolated year in their career, but can they sustain it year after year? The answer is no.

BE ON TOP OF YOUR SALES NUMBERS WEEKLY IF NOT DAILY

Part of the targeting process is to know precisely where you've been, where you are, and where the trends indicate you are going. You need to know what is going on in each of your accounts. Most companies do a good job of providing some sort of daily, weekly, or monthly sales numbers. You must use these numbers to understand where your top accounts are, where the majority of your business is and where your biggest opportunities lie. In addition, sales reports will often show you trends for accounts, indicating where business is increasing or decreasing. If you have a competitive threat in one of your accounts, these reports can give you some idea before it is too late. Hopefully, you will have already known it just by being in the account often enough, but sometimes it's just not possible or obvious.

When I joined J&J in 1990, one of the Senior Sales Reps, Rick Puleo, took the time to not only show me how to review and stay on top of my numbers, but also how to analyze inventory levels of my customer's "custom procedure trays". The old sales rep, who had been promoted, moved on to his new job with the company and quit keeping inventory of the "custom procedure trays" before I arrived. Not to go into a lot of detail, but trust me, this is a very bad thing. Custom trays are very large packs that contain almost all of the disposable products in a surgical procedure. One of the largest trays is the Open Heart Tray, which can contain 50-100 items.

Well, the first day I walked into my new territory, I received a call from my largest account informing me that they ran out of Open Heart Trays and "What was I going to do about it?" This was a nightmare. This was the worst possible thing that could ever happen in the world of custom procedure trays.

Not only were we running the hospital out of open-heart trays, but we were running them out of other trays as well. I soon found out that this guy also had the highest profit margins in the country. This is normally a good thing for companies, but some of his packs were priced

25% higher than the prices our competition was bidding on our business. Once you begin running people out of trays, it's a good possibility the account will begin bidding out your business. Needless to say, we lost that large account within a few months, worth about $750,000. In some companies, $750,000 is an entire territory. Ouch!

During my first few months, Rick took time out of his busy life to show me how to do inventories and to review my monthly numbers. Somehow I managed to salvage the rest of the business in the territory and actually recovered to the point of being runner-up Rookie of the Year. While you get nothing for second place, I was pretty happy with the recovery. Jerry Seinfeld once said, "I would never want to win the Silver Medal in the Olympics because basically of all the losers, you're number one". Basically, I received a pat on the back from my manager, Dave Goldin, and some sympathy. But I also knew that it was because I managed to salvage business in my territory and recovered to the point of having gained enough business back that I was even considered for the award.

Learning how to review my monthly numbers and how to stay on top of my business helped me avoid and defeat many competitive threats. When a particular account didn't produce in a given month, I was alerted to take action. I was able to immediately get into the account and find out what was going on. I could then react and go see customers who could help quell the threat. As we will later discuss, you have to go out and fight these battles rather than hope they will just go away if you want to be a top sales rep.

To summarize this chapter, then:

Set specific goals and WRITE THEM DOWN.
Set goals for every sales call.
Review your sales numbers at least weekly if not daily.

4 BE ENTHUSIASTIC AND GIVE IT YOUR ALL

"The credit belongs to those who are actually in the arena, who strive valiantly; who know the great enthusiasm, the great devotions, and spend themselves in a worthy cause; who at the best, know the triumph of high achievement; and who, at the worst, if they fail, fail while daring greatly, so that their place shall never be with those cold and timid souls who know neither victory nor defeat."

THEODORE ROOSEVELT

"Every great and commanding movement in the annals of the world is the triumph of enthusiasm. Nothing great was ever achieved without it."

RALPH WALDO EMERSON

One of my favorite expressions is, "Successful sales is 65% enthusiasm". Another word for enthusiasm is passion. In this case, however, I am talking about enthusiasm for your products, for your job, and for your company. It only makes sense. Would you rather buy a product from someone who seems bored or unexcited about the products they represent or from someone who really enjoys talking about his wares? I have worked with many reps who knew more about their products then anyone else in their company yet due to their lack of enthusiasm they couldn't sell anywhere near the amount of product other reps sold, who demonstrated more passion and enthusiasm.

One such sale rep was Bill. He was a very nice guy who actually worked in marketing for our company prior to moving into sales. He knew more about the technical aspects of our products than anyone. His customers seemed to like him but when he demonstrated the products you had to put toothpicks in your eyes just to stay awake. He just couldn't sell anything! Most of his problem was simply that he lacked enthusiasm. Not only was he not excited about his products, he seemed to be negative about everything. He was negative about the company, his products, and sometimes his customers; and they knew it. Your customers usually feel this sort of negativity, and you don't even have to verbally communicate it to them. They can see it in your body language and they hear it in your voice.

When you go into a sales call "pump yourself up". Remind yourself that you have the best products in the industry, that you are the best rep, and that you work for the greatest company. Call it affirmations if you like, but you need to be enthusiastic. Your customers will feel your enthusiasm and they will get excited too. Whatever your product, whether it's a cleaning supply or a microchip, get excited about it.

One of my most enjoyable years, in sales management, was working for CORDIS Endovascular. I had a great manager in Jeff Oveland, and the President of the company was Bob Coradini. Enthusiasm overflowed from Bob. He never carried a sales bag in his career, but when you brought Bob into sales calls his enthusiasm was instantly transferred to the customers. They were sold on using your products because they wanted to be a part of the CORDIS family. His enthusiasm was contagious. He really did create a family and that inspired people to do their best. And strive to be great.

I believe that the attitude at the top of an organization filters down into the basic fiber of every company. If there is a lot of back stabbing and politics at the top, then the sales people are going to only look out for themselves and cover their backs. If there is an environment of teamwork and support at the top, then the sales reps will go out of their way to help each other. Make people feel your positive energy and enthusiasm by thinking about it before every call and pumping yourself up. **Make your attitude contagious. Make people remember you and your enthusiasm.**

5 | BE PERSISTENT

"Nothing in this world can take the place of persistence. Talent will not; nothing is more common than unsuccessful men with talent. Genius will not; unrewarded genius is almost a proverb. Education will not; the world is full of educated derelicts. Persistence and determination alone are omnipotent. The slogan "press on" has solved and always will solve the problems of the human race."

CALVIN COOLIDGE

I am not judged by the number of times I fail, but by the number of times I succeed. And the number of times I succeed is in direct proportion to the number of times I can fail and keep trying!

TOM HOPKINS, SALES TRAINER AND WRITER

One of the first sales books I ever read was Tom Hopkins', How to Master the Art of Selling Anything. That book gave me the sales foundation that got me started in my career. I highly recommend you pick up a copy and read it.

Rarely does anyone make the sale on the first call. Many studies have shown that the sale isn't made until the 4th, 5th, 6th, or 7th call. In fact, every book, study, or article I've ever read on this subject, suggests this. So, why do some sales reps take "no" from a customer and never go back? I think it's the fear of rejection or maybe the fact that they don't understand the concept of persistence. There are some sales in which you must close on the first call, such as car sales, but in most sales, persistence is king.

I have seen many sales reps make the mistake of showing a key customer a product, and then they fail to call on them for months or even years because the customer said they weren't interested. This is a terrible mistake. A recently reported study demonstrated that less than 5 percent of the salespeople surveyed continued calling on an account or customer after 6 turndowns. But in many cases, accounts were won or products were sold after the prospect had said, " no" eight times.

I believe that with persistence, you are planting the "seeds" for a future sale, even if you get turned down the first, second, or third time. Certainly, on every call you could and should be closing, as you might just get the sale on the first call. You should be asking for their business or at a minimum asking the customer to do something to move the process to the next step. In some cases, you may be closing for the customer to evaluate a product, or to take the next step in buying your product. But even if they turn you down, you must come back. If you have passion for your product, if you believe in your product, you must go back until they buy.

As a great salesmen and my former Region Director, Jeff Oveland once said, "You must be pleasantly persistent to succeed". What he meant was that persistence is the way to sales success but you must do it in a way that you remain a welcomed visitor.

Keep in mind, you will never be a successful sales rep if you give up easily. While sales can be one of the most rewarding and fun jobs there is, it is also a very tough job. Even if you hear "no", you must continue going back with new ideas, fresh approaches, and new information. At some point, your competitor is going to do something wrong like backordering product, misleading the customer, or something that opens the door for you. But if you quit knocking on that door, how can you walk through it when it finally opens?

Remember, Thomas Edison failed over fifteen hundred times before he succeeded in inventing the incandescent light bulb. He would never consider them failures but rather "1500 ways not to make the light bulb". He learned from each and every attempt, which brought him that much closer to one of the most important inventions of our time. Imagine if he had quit after the first attempt! We might all be sitting in the dark or reading by candlelight.

Here is an email I sent one of my sales teams:

"The biggest mistake many sales reps make is that when they approach a customer and get shot down, they never go back. Each of you has "stone-walled" accounts in your territories as well as customers who want nothing to do with your product. As the great Jimmy Valvano once said, "Never give up. Never give up". Never stop calling on key customers. With persistence, your message will eventually get through or circumstances will change. The competition's rep will leave (due to your persistence), others will eventually irritate the customers, or the competition will take customers for granted. At some point, that difficult Director will finally retire, or that mean Materials Manager will change jobs. The point is, things change but if you don't continue making contact, you lose and your competition wins."

I sent this email to one of my teams and coincidentally, after nine years, one of my reps finally closed a customer on using our products. He had a bad experience with our product years ago and said he would never use it again. That wouldn't deter the rep as he knew we had a great product and that this customer's bad experience was a fluke. After nine years, he got em!

6 HAVE A POSITIVE ATTITUDE AND AN UPBEAT PERSONALITY

"Nothing can stop the man with the right mental attitude from achieving his goal; nothing on earth can help the man with the wrong mental attitude."

PRESIDENT THOMAS JEFFERSON

"A negative mind never attracts happiness or material success, but it will attract the opposites."

NAPOLEON HILL

Always be an upbeat, positive person. Help others to succeed and give credit to those who help you, even if they had very little to do with the sale. It will come back to you ten-fold. Creating positive energy for others will create positive energy for you. I really believe this. But don't always do things expecting something in return. The positive energy may not come back to you for many years down the line, but it will come. So, work towards creating as much positive energy in the world and you will live a positive life.

Those who spend their lives creating negative energy will receive a lot of negative energy back. Negativity creates ill health, disease, and mental anguish; so don't create it. And avoid those who are negative; they aren't healthy to be around.

People enjoy working with others who are positive. They will help you accomplish your goals. No one likes to work with a sad sack; someone who is always negative. If you are a fun, positive person, people will go out of their way to help you.

You can't teach someone to have a great personality but you can be a good salesperson without one. Sure, it makes it much easier if you are fun to be around but you don't have to be the "life of the party". You do need to be someone people like. You may think you have a good personality, but if you are working hard, planning, targeting, goal setting, being a team player, and backing everything with a burning desire and you are STILL not achieving your goals, you may need to do a personality check. The one personality trait that nobody likes is negativity. People run from these types as fast as they can and customers don't like them either.

I would find it hard to believe that you would be doing all the things outlined in this book and still be losing business, but some sales rep's problem is they just "grate" on people's nerves. If you just keep a positive, upbeat outlook, it will do wonders for your personality and relationships, both professional and personal.

Customers, and remember they are people just like you, don't like to be around negative "grouches". If you suspect, for just a minute, that you are repelling people with your personality, you might consider investing in a personal coach. You might also ask the opinions of friends and family as to what things you might improve on with your personality. You might ask your manager to just open up and give you the "full skinny" as to what things they think you should change in your approach or behavior. Ask them to give you their complete, honest, and total feedback on how you can do better. It's a tough step, but if you are struggling and you really want to get better, you must face your fears and get the answers to difficult questions.

When I work with sales reps, I try not to bombard them with a million little details about their personality, approach, sales tactics, etc. I try to pick one or two major things that they can do to highly impact their territories, rather than de-motivate them with 20 things.

There have been some reps with whom I have dreaded spending time. Three days with them in the car, driving around their territory was torture. They not only grated on customers but they grated on me as well. I would love it, sometimes, if they would just say, "Coach, just let me have it. Tell me every single thing I can improve on and I will listen with an open mind, without being defensive". The problem is that most of these people don't seem to realize how bad they are and if you give them the slightest feedback, they get defensive.

Most of the reps and managers that have had a huge impact on my career and outlook, have very positive personalities. Below is a list of the things that I see in common with people possessing GREAT personalities, and who are highly successful. Try and see where you fall within these traits. (Be honest with yourself!)

1) They are **always upbeat and positive.** You can rarely tell if they are having a good day or a bad day. They are high on life and they are usually laughing or smiling during conversations. They are very charismatic and very upbeat. There have been studies conducted on centurions (people who live past the age of 100) and the most common trait they find is their ability to cope with the hardships of life. They are consummate optimists who find the good in everything. So if you want to live over 100, it's time to get positive.

2) They **have a great sense of humor** and people seem to love to be around them. The majority of people who are self-made successes, especially in sales, have fun in their life and in their careers. Even during the tough times, or during tragedy in their lives, they find a way to smile and to maintain their sense of humor.

3) They **sincerely care about people and their customers.** When you see them, they always have a way of making you feel special. They put their hand on your shoulder and give you a firm handshake. They listen intently to what you are saying and you sense they are sincerely interested.

4) They really **don't talk too much about their problems.** If they do, once again, they somehow do it in a positive way. Rather than dwell on their problems, they tend to talk about the opportunities in life, not the challenges.

---

5) They **don't make excuses** for the "hand" they've been dealt. They take responsibility for where they are in life. If they want to make things better, they talk about solutions, not excuses.

6) They **don't gossip or talk negatively about others.** This is a hard one, because many times people and life can seem unfair, but the truly great ones keep negative things about others to themselves. There is a belief in some religions that when you speak badly about someone, or gossip, it is as bad a sin as murder because in a sense you are killing their lives, spirit, and reputation here on earth. In fact, the great sales reps are usually offering sincere praise of others.

7) They are **confident in themselves** and their abilities. Everyone loves to be around a winner. It doesn't mean you have to be "cocky" or arrogant, but take stock in all the positive things about yourself. Realize that there is no one else exactly like you. You will never be someone else either. You can improve your personality, but not everyone can be Albert Einstein, Jerry Seinfeld, Michael Jordan, or Jack Nicholson. Be yourself but that doesn't mean you can't improve yourself.

Many people will say, "Hey, I am who I am and if people don't like it, tough." On the one hand, be happy and confident with who you are, but always strive to be better. You may never be a stand-up comedian, an actor, or a sports star, but you can still strive to be the best at whatever you do. So, be confident in you, but always strive to be a better salesperson and human being.

8) Great sales reps **always do the right things in life.** You don't have to worry about all-around great reps stabbing you or anyone else in the back. They work to get ahead by their own merits and by helping others. They would never hurt others in order to get something for themselves.

9) They inspire you and others. When you are around them, you feel good about yourself. Their success makes you want to learn from them. They make you want to be better. You see in them what you can be. It becomes obvious to you, where and how you can improve.

10) You find that **you want to keep talking to them** because it is **fun, inspiring, uplifting and educational**. Customers feel this way around great sales reps. Customers say they have five minutes to talk but end up talking to them for an hour.

11) When people talk about them, they say complimentary things. You know the type. **You just never hear anyone say anything bad about them.** We should all strive to possess such qualities that people talk about us that way. You don't meet a lot of people like that but I can name a handful. It's a wonderful characteristic. Many people think that in order to get ahead in life, they have to "take care of Number One". They look out for themselves and they don't worry about anyone else. They step on others to move up the ladder. Everyone distrusts them and no one respects them. The truly great sales reps and leaders command the respect of almost everyone. Even people, who dislike them because of jealousy or insecurity, respect and admire them deep down.

12) Top sales people **always see the "glass as half full"**. They are the ultimate optimists. They don't see obstacles in their territories, only opportunities. In fact, when they come up against challenges, they know there is "gold" to be discovered, in figuring out a way around them. I read somewhere that when great sales reps come upon a road block, they figure out a way to a) go over it b) go under it c) go around it or d) go through it. Nothing stops them. They are on a mission and will keep moving forward until they reach success. There is no other option for them. Below average sales people usual choose another option. They choose to retreat.

13) A trait my wife, Alissa, observed in highly successful sales reps and people with great personalities, is they **never argue with their customers**. They may disagree, but somehow they find a way to "plant the seed" without the customer ever knowing it. Somehow, their idea becomes the customer's idea. They say phrases like, "Well, that may be true, but did you consider this? "I can see your point. In addition, what do you think about this?" Somehow they just never directly disagree. They work to avoid confrontation at all cost and they work to gently sway you to their line of thinking.

I'm not sure if I have met someone that possesses 100% of these qualities, 100% of the time. However, we should all strive to grow in these areas. I have met successful people in all walks of life who possess a good majority of them; which is why they are successful. They are the best of the best at whatever they choose to do.

No one likes to be a around a negative, complaining person. I don't need to tell you that. It's a fact of human nature. Do you like to be around a whiner? Most people don't. When you visit customers, you need to brighten up their day; not depress them. I had one rep that worked for me who would go see customers and tell them that he needed them to buy something because he had five kids to feed and he bought a house that was too expensive. Can you imagine?

I'm not making it up. When I went to work with him for the first time, several customers pulled me aside and asked, "What's the deal with your rep? We don't like hearing about all his problems." After working with over 80 reps, I think customers may have directly complained to me about their rep three times. They've got to be pretty bad for a customer to pull a manager aside or call a manager. Most customers just don't want to get involved.

Needless to say, this rep's performance was on the bottom of the pile and he soon left the company. If you wake up one day feeling sorry for yourself, kick yourself in the rear and change your attitude fast. If you don't, you probably won't sell anything that day.

Having taken on a new sales management assignment, one of the tenured reps had only been successful selling our one main product; she was somewhat one-dimensional. When I asked her about selling our other products, she basically said that her customers would never use these products because they were too loyal to the products the people who trained them used. Now how is it that other reps located throughout the country were able to sell our full line of products but in this one territory it couldn't be done because her customers were somehow different?

Next, I asked her how things were going with our customer incentive program, whereby accounts were offered significant discounts for buying bulk orders. She replied, "Can't be done in this territory. No one will ever go for that sort of program in which they have to lay out $70,000 - $100,000." Once again, reps were utilizing this program all over the country except in this specific territory. Yet, to quote her again, "it can't be done".

So, I tried another approach. I asked her about our other specialty product and why she hadn't been able to sell it. She replied, "there is no one in my territory doing a technique that would call for this product so I can't sell any here". Very interesting since she lives in one of the largest cities in the country, with several major teaching institutions! Yet, to quote her one more time, "it can't be done." There is no word in the English language that I hate more than the word, can't.

I have had many discussions, with reps over the years, but I have never had such a negative dialogue with anyone in my career quite like that. The good news is that as time went on, she became more positive in her outlook and began selling all our products. In fact, she also pulled off some of the most impressive sales accomplishments I have ever witnessed. My feeling is that as a sales rep, you should look around and ask yourself some hard questions:

➤ Are there other reps selling these products?
➤ Could they possibly have challenges as difficult as mine, even if they are different than mine?
➤ Even if a particular approach is not common, are there at least a few customers using it?

➤   While some customers in my area may use one product or approach, couldn't they be taught or exposed to other approaches?

➤   Could it be that while most people would not be interested in a bulk order of products, could there be some that might be interested?

These questions are the same no matter what you are selling. Quit making excuses as to why no one in your territory would be interested in your product and create the interest. If no one is doing a technique or process, that others are finding beneficial, then teach the customers yourself. You will bring value to their business and their loyalty will increase towards you and your company.

What it boils down to is an Attitude with a capital "A". Open up your mind. Don't be negative. Believe in the possibilities and don't limit yourself. Don't be one-dimensional. The truly great reps aren't one-dimensional but rather they are multi-dimensional. They uncover every stone. They pull all the products out of the bag and they get themselves excited about most of them, not just one.

When you remain positive and you help others, you will be amazed at how much people go out of their way to help you if you are nice to them, take an interest in them, and treat them with respect. But the key to it all is to be sincere about it, without the intention of getting something in return.

The following was a passage from an email I sent one of my sales teams on this subject:

"If you have a pleasing, upbeat personality, your customers will respond to you in a positive manner. If you are negative, they will respond to you in a negative manner. Choose to be excited about your company. Choose to be excited about your marketplace. Choose to be excited that God has blessed you with another day on earth. Choose to be excited about the fact that we live in the greatest country in the world. A positive attitude is a choice you can make every day, as is a negative attitude. See the glass half full and it will eventually overflow with successful endeavors."

Another email to one of my teams:

"Choose to associate and communicate with those who can help you raise your level of performance even higher. Don't get pulled down into the "mire" by those who want to see you fail. As I have observed people throughout my career, those who are performing below average always complain about the company, about the comp plan, about the products, about their customers, or about the weather. Choose to be positive and happy, and you will be. Avoid those that will pull you into their world of negativity."

As I mentioned in the last chapter, I once saw a PBS special on centurions. The common thread they shared was their unwavering positive mental attitude and their ability to recover from tragedy in their lives. I have a Great Uncle Harry who is now 95 and going strong. You have never met a more positive, jovial guy in your life. Even when there were tough times, you'd never know it by this guy. When I speak to him, I spend at least 15 minutes listening to his jokes. He's as sharp as a tack and I believe he'll live over 100 because of his positive attitude.

I happen to believe that a Positive Mental Attitude can sometimes prevent and even cure disease. Now, if it can do that, imagine what a good attitude can do for your career! While it's not a guarantee, a positive attitude certainly helps. Each day I must remind myself to stay positive. It's not always easy with all the negative things going on around us, war, traffic, pollution, etc. But, I stop and remind myself about all that is positive in our lives....our families, our country, our companies, our products, the people with whom we work, our good health and on and on and on. Today, I saw a blind man with one of those wonderful Labrador seeing-eye dogs. It's those moments that put things into perspective.

One of the most inspiring stories I have read in a long time was that of Bethany Hamilton. This was the 14 year-old girl who lost her arm in a shark attack. Within three months, she was back surfing without her arm. She believes that it was in God's plan so that others with handicaps could look at her and be inspired. She inspires me, she humbles me; she embarrasses me. How I could let some of the little things in life to EVER get me down is unacceptable. We should all learn the power of positive thinking from this remarkable girl.

7 | HAVE HIGH AMBITION: SET YOUR GOAL TO BE AT THE TOP

*"Life's battles don't always go
To the stronger or faster man;
But sooner or later, the man who wins
Is the one who thinks he can".*

C.W. LONGENBECKER

"Whatever you are; be a good one."

ABRAHAM LINCOLN

With apologies to Mr. Lincoln, let me paraphrase his quote and say, "Whatever you are; be a **great** one!" If you want to be a top salesperson or money earner, you must not only want to be the best at what you do, but one of your top goals must be to obtain the top spot in your sales force. And remember, WRITE IT DOWN!

Yes, every once in a while, someone devises a flawed ranking system in which some of the highest paid sales reps are not the highest ranked, but most of the time the two go together. I have never seen a sales rep who doesn't care about succeeding, end up being a top sales rep on a consistent basis. It goes back to my earlier chapter on WRITTEN, SPECIFIC GOALS. You must set the written goal to be the best if you want to become the best. Having it up, tucked away in your brain, is not going to make it happen. Write down and commit to yourself "I will be Sales Rep of the Year or I will be in the Top 10%".

In addition, you can set the goal to be #1 or in the Top 10%, but you must back that goal with sincerity and a burning desire to actually achieve the goal. Sure, every rep tells me they want to be in the Top 10 or #1, because that's what they think I want to hear, but very few write it down as a goal and then take action to make it happen.

Make it your goal to be the best and commit it to writing.

8 | WORK HARD, GO THE EXTRA MILE AND ADD VALUE TO YOUR CUSTOMERS

"I'm a great believer in luck and I find that the harder I work, the more I have of it."

THOMAS JEFFERSON

"One of my favorite sayings I got off a soda bottle: No Deposit, No Return."

JOHN NABER, FOUR-TIME OLYMPIC GOLD MEDALLIST

While written, specific goals will help you reach success faster than you ever thought possible, "good 'ole fashion" hard work is a requirement for most successful people as well. Only one of the 80-odd sales reps I've managed over the years rose to the top without actually working all that hard. But he made up for that by focusing only on business that would fall easily, and there was a lot of "low-hanging fruit" in his territory. Most of us are neither that focused nor that lucky.

It's important to have some balance in life. However, if you interviewed 100 top sales reps or 100 very successful people, you would find that most of them worked extremely hard to get to that position. At some point, you may get so good and efficient at what you do that you can work less. But almost always you will have to work harder than the "Average Joe" if you want to be the best.

Show me a top rep whose sales performance has declined, and I'll usually show you someone who has, for whatever reason, lost his

49

or her passion for the job. They may be bored or they have started a side business. Maybe they are having problems at home. Whatever the reason, it's usually something that has changed their attitude and work ethic.

Many sales people fail because they just don't get out of bed and go see customers each day. They sit at their desks, move paperwork around, and procrastinate. To be a great sales person, you must take action. You must go see as many customers as you can. Unless you have a manager that micromanages, you may think no one will know how many calls you make, how long you take for lunch, if you are golfing every afternoon, or going to the local bar. But that isn't true. Someone will know. YOU will know.

Eventually, if you aren't working hard and doing the right things, your numbers will "slide" and your little secret will be uncovered. If you want to be successful, you've got to get out and see the customers. As my friend and former manager, Rick Puleo used to say, "just go see customers and pull the products out of the bag". What's amazing is how many sales reps go to see customers and fail to "pull the products out of the bag"; and to get them in the hands of the customers. Some reps fail to even show customers a brochure. Sales reps need to be selling; not just driving around shaking people's hands with the hope that customers will just ask for our products.

When you are driving home at 4:00, you've been out and about since 6:00 am, and you're just plain tired, you should push yourself to go to see one more customer. First of all, customers like people who work hard. Secondly, many times you can catch people at the end of the day, whereas they may not have seen you in the middle of the day. The same holds true for getting out very early in the morning and being the first one to hit the streets. If you get in to see a customer at 6:30 am, they may decide they aren't going to see any more sales reps for the rest of the day. You made it because you made the extra effort to get there early.

I used to go in to see customers on the weekends and cheer up the weekend staff. I might bring in pizza and just "hang out" with them. Many large hospitals have surgery going on 24/7, and reps that make the effort to go in when no one else will, reap tremendous benefits. Things are usually much more relaxed and the customers are much more open to hearing about your products on the weekends or during the night shifts. This is especially valuable when you are first getting started trying to establish relationships and build trust. It doesn't matter what you are selling. If you are selling cleaning supplies and make the effort to go see the weekend crew at the local factory, you will be appreciated, you will make friends, and you will sell product.

Another one of my top 10%'ers, and a selling machine, Terry Bates, used to drive one of his customers from San Diego to Orange County every couple of weeks, when he was doing surgery at his northern hospital. Terry did it for several reasons. One, the customer enjoyed his company and not having to drive himself in traffic. Two, it gave Terry 90 minutes of solid "alone" time, allowing him to build his relationship and sell his products. Needless to say, Terry bagged about 85% of this guy's business, which was phenomenal. Terry also had about 85% market share in his territory, which was almost unheard of in that business.

Look around. Observe how you are treated as a customer and you will realize that with so many average people out there, it really doesn't take a lot to surpass your customer's expectations and to shine. Go the extra mile, and you will outsell most of your competition.

Many studies have been done to determine the amount of time sales reps actually spend in front of customers. What do you think the number is? 70% of their time? 60%? 50%? Guess again. Sales reps, on average, spend only 20-30% of their available time with customers actually selling. It seems hard to believe? What if you could increase that time to 40%, 50%, or 60%? Do you think your sales will go up?

The more things you can do to get yourself face-to-face with a customer, the more successful you will be. Remember, you never sell anyone anything sitting in your office or during drive time to the account. So when you catch yourself procrastinating, get up off your rear end and go see a customer. In fact, put a big sign in your office that says, "Quit procrastinating. Go see a customer!" If your product could be sold at home, in your office, in your car, or on the cell phone, your company could just hire telemarketers and save a lot on commission and overhead. As the old saying goes, "if it were that easy you could just tie a note around a St. Bernard's collar and send it in to get an order for the products."

Any time you begin a new sales job, take over a new sales territory, or start a project, you must work extra hard during those first six months to a year. It's like getting a plane off the ground. You must build up tremendous momentum and speed on the runway and once you get off the ground, you can back off the throttle and the job gets much easier. If you only taxi down the runway at 30 miles per hour, you'll never take off. Thus, starting a new sales job, you must get focused and work extremely hard, get momentum and sales going, and then you can eventually ease back a little.

In sales, you must focus 100% of your attention on getting your "territory" off the ground. I've seen many sales reps who have so many other things going on in their lives that they can't focus on their job. Of course they have their families, which certainly is an important priority. But then they start day trading, or they start a side business. I had one rep I "inherited", who was buying and selling real estate on the side. Not as a part time hobby, maybe selling one house every one or two years, but who was actively doing it as a part time business. It wasn't long before I found out about his secret and he soon left the company.

So, remember, you must stay focused on one thing and work extremely hard. Otherwise, your "plane" will just sputter off the runway, into the weeds or worse, "off the cliff".

It's not uncommon to take over a territory that was "run into the ground" by the previous rep. Because of this, at first, the customers may hate your company, your products, and even you. But, with hard work, drive and persistence, you will eventually win them over. As Henry Ford once said, "When everything seems to be going against you, remember that the airplane takes off against the wind, not with it."

But always keep in mind that while people realize you are a salesperson, they don't want to feel as though all you care about is selling them something. You need to constantly look for ways to add value to their business. Educate them by bringing them training videos, speakers or in-services. When you help them do their job better, you have a friend and customer for life.

There was a man by the name of Roy Dyment, a doorman at the Four Seasons Hotel in Ontario, Canada. One day, a hotel guest exited the hotel and asked Roy to get him a cab. An hour after the attorney left, Roy found the man's briefcase sitting by the curb. He called the man's office and found him in a panic and desperate because the following day he was to give a presentation to a Senate Committee and he needed the papers in the briefcase to do it.

Roy clocked out, changed his clothes, rushed to the airport, bought a round-trip ticket to Washington, D.C. and personally delivered the briefcase to the attorney at his office. Roy was later awarded Employee of the Month, Employee of the Year, and eventually elected into the company's national hall of fame. Now, do you think that attorney thinks twice about staying in any other hotel than a Four Seasons?

In the National Football League, they often say that the difference between the winners and losers is very small. I believe this holds true in sales as well. Be happy with average and you will be average. Insist on being the best and you will be the best. It doesn't take that much more to get there. **Work harder than your competition, and you will be the best.**

9 | HAVE FAITH AND BELIEF

"And it will be, if you will diligently obey My commandments which I enjoin upon you this day, to love the Lord your God and to serve Him with all your heart and with all your soul, I will give rain for your land at the proper time, the early rain and the late rain, and you will gather in your grain, your wine and your oil. And I will give grass in your fields for your cattle, and you will eat and be sated."

THE BIBLE

From observations, experience, and education, I wrote this book to lay out the things I believe are required to not just be a good sales rep, but what it takes to become a great sales rep. If you're not a religious person, or this "stuff" makes you uncomfortable, then skip to Chapter 10. I have found that my faith has made me a better man and a better sales rep. So I hope you will read this chapter.

I believe very strongly in the existence of God; in the potential of this wonderful world and I believe in myself. I truly feel that I would not have achieved all that I have, without that belief and faith. You can achieve almost anything you set your mind to. I say almost anything, because I knew from a very young age, that being white and 5'8", I would never be an NBA All-star basketball player, so you've got to be realistic. Many kids waste their lives chasing a sport or entertainment dream they really have no chance of obtaining. By all means, if you have the talent, go after your dream. Just insure you get an education to back yourself up if you fail.

However, when it comes to most other goals, if you believe in yourself, if you work hard, you have faith, and if you strive to improve yourself, you will succeed. It's interesting to note, that one of the people who pre-read this book felt I should remove any reference of God as many might find it offensive or too deep for some. Now, isn't that a sad state of affairs? I feel that the more faith we have in this world, in ourselves, in our fellow man, and in God, the more incredible things we can accomplish as a human race, not only as individuals but also as a world community.

I don't think anyone is awarded things in this world because they pray. I don't think football teams win games over an opponent because they prayed for it, but I do believe that those who strive to be better, and ask for the strength and wisdom to achieve their goals, will be successful in most of their endeavors. It won't be easy and there will be many roadblocks and challenges, but faith and belief will keep you on the path to success.

Success also requires a positive mental attitude. If you feed your subconscious with negative thoughts, negative things will happen. If you have faith in yourself, in God, and in your fellow man, positive things will happen. When you are under pressure, competition is steep, and you are about to give up; don't. Have faith in yourself and God, and push forward and amazing things will happen. I think it's always important, when we are out their everyday, to keep things in perspective; to think about the "big picture" and to have our priorities set in the right order.

I also believe that there is a solution to every problem in this universe. I don't believe there are any shortages of resources in this world. Thus, if we, as humans, focus on these problems and roadblocks, and back that focus with faith and belief, eventually the solutions and ideas to solve these problems will come to us. This applies to you and your sales career as well. I have almost always believed that I would succeed in everything I have attempted. It was only those few times when I had doubt that I did not succeed.

When you're having a tough day, pull out a dollar bill, and you'll find the words, "In God We Trust". Think about it for a moment and remember that there are bigger things happening in this world and the fact that someone cut you off in traffic, or you missed a sale, might seem a little less important. Hopefully it will also remind you to have a little faith.

I feel it is extremely important, no matter how tough it get's, to tithe 10% of your earnings to charity. Not only is it the right thing to do, but it will come back to you ten-fold, both mentally and physically. You cannot understand the power of this until you do it consistently over time. In fact, 10% of the income from this book will be going straight to worthy causes.

10 | WORK SMART. DO WHAT IS IMPORTANT TO SELL PRODUCTS

Nature gave men two ends, one to sit on and one to think with. Ever since then man's success or failure has been dependent on the one he used most often.

GEORGE KILPATRICK

I must govern the clock, not be governed by it.

GOLDA MEIR FORMER ISRAELI PRIME MINISTER

Run your territory. Don't let it run you!

DAVE GOLDIN, TOP SALES MANAGER, J&J

As a newcomer in medical sales, the first words of advice I received were "Run your territory. Don't let it run you". This bit of wisdom, which has stayed with me ever since, was offered by my good friend, manager, mentor, and a truly great sales rep, Dave Goldin, when I first joined Johnson & Johnson. Dave went on to say, "Dean, you're going to have opportunity every day. You will have so much opportunity; you will not know where to begin. Customers will be calling you to fix this problem and fix that problem. They will want new catalogues, price lists, samples and brochures. They're going to demand that you come see them now and straighten things out immediately."

"Most people would look at these things as hassles. You must look at them as opportunities. You've got to prioritize. You can't always drop what you are doing to bring someone a catalogue, so you've got to work with your customer to manage your time. Just be sure to run your territory and don't let your territory run you."

Because Dave possesses such a positive outlook, he calls things other people consider problems, "opportunities". That's because he knows that every time you come into contact with customers, things can happen and products can be sold. One minute you are providing service, but you pull out your new products and "BAM", you have another opportunity to sell.

That's why you need to focus, and insure you close business, not just drum up interest. You must stop, prioritize and go after the "low hanging fruit". When your customer calls and asks you to handle a situation, you must call them back immediately. You must ask yourself and the customer "Do I need to come out today, or can I get out tomorrow or in a few days?"

You don't want to blow people off. You want to always provide excellent service and follow-up, you just need to make sure your customers don't run you ragged if it is OK to wait a day or two. That way you can maximize your valuable time. The more you can minimize "windshield time" and put yourself in front of customers, the more products you will sell and the more money you will make.

If you're a good sales rep, you care about your customers. They know you do. They sense it. But often, there are just too many customers to cover in your monthly call schedule. There is only so much time in the day. You must work smart and do the things that will give you the biggest "bang for the buck" without ignoring any of your customers. It is very important that you identify your existing top accounts, and if you're in an industry that doesn't provide repeat business, you must identify your top prospects. In any type of industry or environment, you must *focus on the top prospects*.

PRIORITIZE YOUR OPPORTUNITIES

Many sales reps work by the seat of their pants, and work every account for new business. It's important to weigh the upside of an account and the energy it takes to gain that business. There is a point of diminishing returns in which small prospects or accounts just aren't worth the amount of time and energy to gain their business.

But also keep in mind that sometimes it takes very little to convert business in a small account. It's not that these customers are "easy"; it's just that so many reps ignore them and never come around. When you show an interest in them, they are more than willing to give you some business. I don't want to "waffle" on my point, but the fact is you must analyze each situation. If you can easily convert a small account, do it; just don't waste a lot of time doing it. Once you do convert the account, they deserve great quality service as well. They won't require quite as much to remain happy, as those "spoiled" large accounts, but call on them periodically, just to let them know you are there for them and not taking them for granted.

The reality is that if you are in a very difficult territory, in which the large accounts are locked up pretty tight, your initial strategy may be to convert some small accounts while still banging on the door of the large accounts. If you have an "earth shattering" technology or your competition is weak, your best strategy will be to focus on the large accounts. Every territory is different.

When you do actually go out to physically see small accounts, to answer a question or provide service, make sure you use the opportunity to show them products as well. Don't let any call be wasted.

In short, small accounts shouldn't be your highest priority, but at the same time, you should never ignore a customer; even a small one. Sometimes, small customers can become big accounts. Whereas one year they might be doing very little business, things may change. Another company might acquire them. Or, in the case of hospitals, a new physician might come in who already uses your products. They may begin doing a tremendous amount of procedures. If you ever failed to return their phone call or said you would show up and didn't, you'll be waiting a long time trying to get their business now.

Another thing – people move. That person in the small account you ignore today, could be the decision-maker in a much bigger account tomorrow. Once again, by ignoring them when they had a less important position or when they were at the smaller account, you've now shot yourself in the foot. On the other hand, if you gave them good service when they were at a small account, they won't forget it when they move up in life.

I always made it a point to return every customer's phone call immediately and, if they needed information or support, react within a reasonable amount of time. I may not have been able to get there the next day but I would certainly make it there within a week. I also made it a point to be honest and upfront with them. The worst thing you can do is tell a customer that you will be there on a certain day, at a certain time, and just not show up.

In addition, it's a small world and word travels. Rick Puleo, one of the best in the business, used to always tell us to "under-promise and over-deliver". This way you will always delight your customers. If you "over-promise and under-deliver", you won't gain their trust or their business. If you already have it, you'll soon lose it.

One of my competitors was once caught stealing a purchase order from an account and shipping in product under that stolen P.O. number. He did it to win a year-end trip. How low will someone go? Not only was he banned from that account, but those customers talked to other accounts. He lost business all over his territory from that single dishonest act. And he was never trusted by anyone in that part of his territory ever again.

My brother David, as he heard this story, asked, "Why wasn't this guy fired?" Well, in the short term, life isn't always just. I have seen incompetent, dishonest, evil people float along in companies for years. Everyone around them would be asking, "What does this person have "on" someone that allows them to keep their job?" We all just shake our heads in amazement. But, what experience has also taught me is that eventually it all catches up with them. It may take two, five, or ten years but eventually they get what they deserve.

Most people, during my career, have treated me extremely well, but those that were unjust to me or others were all eventually fired. It's almost amazing to look back and see how things ended up. During the time these people "hang on", sometimes for years, everyone is questioning the fairness of it all. But I believe everything happens for a reason. I feel I learned almost as much about how not to behave professionally or how not to sell, from these bad apples, as I learned the right way to do things or to behave from the great ones.

REVIEW YOUR SALES REPORT FOR TRENDS

Another way to work smart and to focus is to "be on top of your sales numbers" as we discussed earlier. To discuss in more detail, every month, I would print off my variance report on the Saturday after the month-end close. I would sit by the pool, and look to see what product codes were down in each account. I would look at the variance report and when I saw that an account had a variance, I would study the 12 month rolling report for the ordering patterns. If I had any doubt or concern that they had switched any code or any large piece of business, I would visit the account that next Monday. I would look for clues or competitive product on the shelves, or note what products were being pulled. Were they mine?

Finally, I would ask the customers whether they were evaluating competitive product, and if so, why. Many customers will tell you that everything is fine, if you ask them on the phone. That's why it's important to go into the account and verify it personally, "in the flesh". No one likes to tell someone bad news. Also, they may not want you coming in to disrupt their competitive evaluation, but you've got to defend your business. If you ask a top rep about one of their accounts, they can immediately tell whatever you want to know.

It's twice as hard to gain back business you've lost, as it is to win it in the first place. And waiting to react to a competitive threat only makes it worse.

If you hold back and wait a few months before you respond to a competitive challenge, you're sunk. Materials Management now has the leverage to say to the end users, "hey, you've used the new product successfully for three months, now why, all of a sudden, is there a problem with it?

CONSTANTLY RE-SELL YOUR PRODUCTS

Another way to work smart is to constantly "re-sell" your products to your customers. "Re-selling your products"; continually showing the customers the clinical or support data; and reminding them of the features and benefits for which they converted to your products in the first place will put a "fence around your business". You will prepare your customers for the misleading information your competitors may provide. Whenever new data becomes available, make sure they see it. Otherwise, your competitors will take that same information and try and distort it in such a way that they will convert your business to their products.

No matter what product you sell, you must constantly remind them as to why they are using your product. For example, if you sell computer software you must make sure you let your customers know about upgrades, or new versions before your competitors get into your accounts, show them their new, next generation software and take your business. You might have an even better version then theirs but you failed to let the customer know and they have now gone down the road with the new guys. The same hold true with virtually any product.

This is a trap that many older, long-term sales reps fall into. They work their territories for so long and know so many people that they relax. They start to take things for granted. They quit selling and fall into the "maintain the relationship mode". They tend to spend a lot of time golfing with customers or entertaining. But in many industries, this only takes you so far. For many companies, especially during recessions, cost will become an issue. When you are under competitive threat, you will tend to fall into a "save the business mode", which is just another way of saying "panic mode". Panic mode isn't a good thing. When you are in the panic mode, customers view you as desperate. They'll question your data, or worse, your motives. They may feel you are crying over "spilled milk", undermining the relationship you worked so hard to develop.

If you haven't been re-selling your products continually, your competition will have brainwashed your customers before you even know there is a threat!

This doesn't need to happen. If you have been re-selling your product in a "pleasantly persistent way" all along, your customers will "go to bat" for you on a technical or clinical basis. They will go to the material managers, buyers, CEO's, or CFO's and explain why it would be penny wise and pound foolish to switch from your products to your competitor's.

Relationships only go so far. You must constantly defend the value of your product to your customers. Unfortunately, many long-term reps get out of practice doing this. It's not always fun, so they often tend to blame their companies, the economy, or the changes in their territory as to why they are losing business, rather than admit that they just hadn't been "re-selling" their products. It's always the tenured reps that complain when companies want to put all the reps through sales training courses. But the fact is that many times it is those tenured reps that really need the "brush up" the most.

Even the best athletes in the world go back basic to training. I was told that Vince Lombardi used to always say at the beginning of spring training, "Gentlemen, this is a football". Sounds funny, but his point was that whether you are an athlete or a salesman, you must always go back to the basics if you want to be a winner.

LOOK FOR WAYS TO SAVE TIME

Another way to work smart is to look for ways to save time. The greatest way to save time is to go back to the chapter on writing goals. If you take 15 minutes a day to review your goals, update them, and work out the next day's steps to achieve those goals, you will save many hours a week. You will be much more efficient and you will avoid wasting time. You will call ahead to ensure your appointments are still scheduled. You will avoid calling on people who really have very little potential or authority to buy your product and who always seem to be the ones who love to talk.

A great way to realize how much time you waste is to document, for a few days, every moment of your day. It doesn't take long to realize that you may be wasting a tremendous amount of time. By the same token, a great way to eliminate those time wasters is to plan every minute of the day.

Most reps spend too much time in their offices. They procrastinate. They push paper around on their desk. They focus on the unimportant things on their "To Do List". They do everything they can to avoid getting out to see customers and face the possibility of rejection.

They always seem to be the reps with the most impressive power point presentations and all you asked for was a five-minute talk on filling out expense reports! I believe that any sales rep whose presentations are too detailed are spending too much time in their office. Let marketing put together fancy presentations for you to use. Your job is to be face to face with customers, showing and selling products.

All sales jobs are challenging and hard but they are also incredibly rewarding. If I had a dollar for every time I have heard the expression "Work Smart", I'd be retired. The fact is, to keep up with all the opportunity in this world, you've got to work smart. It's just so important, if you want to be a top sales rep or be the best at whatever you do.

Skipping an appointment is the kiss of death. Its even worse if you are so rude as to not call in plenty of time to warn them. Manage your time. Don't make appointments you can't keep, especially with people who are hard to see. You may never get another appointment with them again. If you are running late, let them know. Showing up 30 minutes late, hoping they forgive you is a bad strategy. No one, let me say it again, *no one* likes to wait. Not for a date, not for a dinner with friends, not for *anything*. So, why in the world would you make it a habit of being late for people who directly impact the income you earn to put food on your table?

Plan your schedule. I like to work backwards from an appointment, and schedule time for each activity leading up to it, leaving ample time for each activity. For example, let's take the first appointment of the day. The first thing I do, of course, is put the appointment in my daily planner in pencil, and then I work backwards, putting in drive time and padding for extra discussion. Do what works for you but be sure to plan. As it's often said, "Plan your work. Then work your plan".

There are always plenty of phone calls and follow-up you need to work through in a day. By leaving plenty of time to get where you are going, you also leave yourself time to knock off those "non-selling" and phone follow-ups. Your schedule during the day is like a daily goals list. If you write down your goals, you will be more likely to accomplish them.

DO WHAT IS IMPORTANT & WHAT YOU KNOW TO BE RIGHT

Many times, those in the home office believe they know what is right for your customers. But you are the one in the trenches and you must stand up for what you believe is right. Sometimes that can be hard, especially if you are fairly new with the company. In addition, there will be times when upper management will suggest or will tell you to do something, which you know is wrong. When that happens you must stand up and be heard. At least if you express your opinion, and the business "goes south", you won't be blamed. If the company believes you must hold price or margins then that is a business decision that they have chosen and you can live with that.

I'm not telling you to be a troublemaker. I'm saying that you should work with your manager, keep him or her in the loop, present things in a business and professional manager, and make sure the company HEARS your opinion. Don't wimp out. They will respect you for it. Just don't always think about *me, me, me.* If you get tagged as someone who only cares about yourself, people will stop wanting to help you. Sometimes, what you think is right doesn't fall into the company policies. If you stated your case, sometimes you must just walk away from business and be supportive of the company policies or pricing strategies.

Many times, the company wants you to let them know what's happening in "the field" and if you fail to speak up, and business is lost, that may put you in a difficult situation. Make a business case. Your manager and upper management will respect the fact that you understand the account, the opportunities, and the risks. You have laid them out and presented them in a proposal. The company may decide to reject your proposal but at least you spoke up.

When I first began my career, I was very excited and somewhat intimidated by it all. After all that work to get the job, I was so happy to be with such a great company and to be once again employed, that if they told me to run through a brick wall, I would have done it. I believed that many of the people above me had been in this business for a long time and that surely they knew the right thing to do in various situations. Who was I to question them? I just did what was asked of me and in many respects, that was a good thing.

However, sometimes, in your heart, you know something is wrong. That's when you must really speak up. As I progressed in my career, gained more confidence in the job I was doing, I became rapidly more successful. I learned that I needed to take control of my business. As long as you present things in a positive, professional manner, and as a business case, rather than as a panic response, your company and manager will respect you. They should, at a minimum, listen to your proposal or action plan.

To illustrate this point, let me describe one of the most difficult situations I faced, as a new sales rep. A few chapters back, I discussed the importance of knowing where your business is and where it is going. I described my nightmare with "custom procedure trays". Also, as I mentioned, these big packs provide almost all the disposable products for a surgical procedure. In the past, hospitals would buy each individual product and put them on the shelf in the operating room. Each morning hospital personnel would pick each product, individually, that would be needed in each specific surgical procedure.

At some point, some creative individual came up with the idea of providing a giant pack that contained the majority of products that would be needed. By using lower cost labor, and cutting back on the number of purchase orders that would need to be "cut" for all those products, as well as many other cost efficiency reasons, "custom trays" became the standard in most busy hospitals.

When I was in the business, we would go in at a competitive price, allowing us to earn a reasonable profit. Our competitors would "bid" the custom trays at "below cost", knowing that over time they could 1) switch more expensive products, that the customer asked for initially, for cheaper products or 2) they could remove products they saw being wasted or unused, without lowering the cost or only lowering it for a nickel, when it cost the manufacturer a dollar. All these "tricks" allowed those companies that "bid" below cost, to raise their margins quite substantially over time.

My company would not allow themselves to be pulled down to this level of game playing and underhanded tactics. As the business became more and more of a bid "game" versus being able to sell on quality assurance, customer service, etc. and was only focused on price, it became very unprofitable.

I began right at a time when the bidding wars for custom trays and all the games were being played. I inherited a territory from a guy who gained business at a large hospital on the West Coast of Florida. His profit margins were extremely high. I knew it and I believe that the customer realized it as well.

About two months on the job, this account, the same one we ran out of heart trays, informed me that they would be "bidding" our "trays" out to all the other companies. I immediately contacted my manager, who called the home office to find out what we might do, now that our high prices were exposed. Their solution was to get the hospital on a "plant tour" so that we could show them our high quality products and manufacturing techniques, justifying our premium price.

After telling the customer, she responded, "Dean, we know your company makes fine products. That is one reason we gave them a contract in the first place, but we also know that Baxter and Sterile Concepts make fine products as well." My boss called the home office and again the advice to us was to get them on a plant tour. Now, in my heart, I knew this was a mistake as they were very adamant about not wanting to go on a plant tour. But I was panicked and desperate for upper management's guidance and wisdom. I didn't want to do the wrong thing but at the same time, I wanted to be a good soldier.

After asking about three times for them to go on a plant tour, I almost got banned out of the account. The material manager called me into her office and said, "We don't like pushy sales reps. We don't want to go on a plant tour, and if you keep pushing us, you won't be allowed into the hospital." I was devastated. First of all, I knew I was persistent but I certainly wasn't pushy. My other customers would attest to that.

So, after only three months on the job, we lost all that business because the competition bid the product at 50% lower than our price.

The good news is that we got out of the custom tray business and by the time I was promoted a few years later, I had converted almost every "stitch" of other possible business, in that account. As I look back, it was probably one of my favorite and greatest accomplishments as a sales rep.

The moral of the story is that I should have strongly told the company sooner, that the plant tour idea was a bad idea. While I still think we would have lost the business, I would not have had to work so hard to repair the damage and regain my reputation. Management really needed me to step up and tell them what we needed to do. Only three months into the job, I was too unsure of myself to do it. You've got to try and avoid this mistake.

BE PREPARED AND ORGANIZED

Sometimes, you'll only have two minutes with a customer. They may not have wanted to see you in the first place but they go ahead and give you two minutes. There's nothing more frustrating to a customer, than a sales rep that begins fumbling around trying to find brochures, samples, or studies when they didn't really want to see them in the first place.

To prevent that from happening, never make a sales call without your detail bag, brochures, clinical papers and demos. All these tools need to be organized and easily identified inside your DETAIL BAG so that you can quickly get them out. In an earlier chapter, we learned that you need identified goals and outcomes for each sales call. If you do that, you should know exactly what you want to talk to that customer about and you should already have a package of information ready. If you end up talking about another product, that shouldn't be a problem. Simply grab the brochure for that product. You should also have your demo kits ready to go. Don't be assembling things during your two-minute visit. As we will discuss in other chapters, if you are good at asking solid, open ended questions, and getting the demos into your customers hands, your two minute discussion can turn into fifteen.

11 | DON'T PROCRASTINATE. GET YOUR ACT TOGETHER AND HAVE A SENSE OF URGENCY.

"Some men dream of worthy accomplishments, while others stay awake and do them."

BERNARD EDMONDS

"There are three kinds of people in this world: There's those people that make things happen, those people that watch things happen, and those people that don't know what's happening.

JOHN MADDEN, FORMER COACH
OF THE CHAMPION OAKLAND RAIDERS

What type of person are you?

DON'T PROCRASTINATE

Great sales people seize the day. They don't wait until tomorrow. They step up to the plate and swing at the ball. They take action. They don't procrastinate. They are willing to take chances and they don't spend a lot of time waiting for the "perfect moment". *They have a sense of urgency* in everything they do and they always have their act together.

Poor sales reps procrastinate and they don't have a sense of urgency in life or in their careers. When they fail, they blame everyone and everything else for their failure. "It's my manager"; "It's my territory"; "It's the type of customers I have". I always say that if failing sales reps would spend as much time and energy in self-reflection as they do looking for excuses, they wouldn't be failing.

There are several things about procrastination you need to know. First, many new reps want to wait until they are experts on every aspect of their products, before they get out, see customers, and show them what they have. If you do that, three months may pass and by the time you get out of your office, your territory may already be "going south". While you are sitting at your desk becoming an "expert", your competitors are out there selling products. So GET OUT THERE.

You should learn as much as you can during your sales training period, which is normally during your first 2-8 weeks of a new job. Once training is complete and you are let loose on your own, you need to hit the streets immediately. Keep your education going at night and on weekends, until you become an expert, but don't spend weeks in your office, during selling time, trying to become an expert.

During the initial training period, you need to take advantage of that time out of the territory, to learn as much as you can. This way, you will be that much closer to being the expert, before you ever get back home. If your company sends you pre-reading material to prepare for the classroom, then you need to work hard and read it. Watch the videos or CD's they send you and be as prepared for the "in-house" training as much as you possibly can. Otherwise, there may be others in the class with more knowledge or experience. Don't slow the rest of the class down because you came unprepared and don't slow yourself down.

When you are at the training course during your first few weeks, learn as much as you can. You need to study in the evenings, either alone or with study groups at night, versus going out on the town and partying. This is your livelihood and your family is depending on you. You need to do well in training so that you can hit the ground running and NOT take three months to start making an impact.

Some reps might not give it their all in training, and so they spend the first weeks in their territories, trying to get up to speed. These are the same guys, who after the group study sessions each night or during training, move on to the hotel bar until all hours and show up to class like zombies. This is a big mistake. Sales is a numbers game and the clock is ticking. Your manager hired you because he or she believed you would be a "winner" and would help their team to be the best. They're depending on you as well, as is your family.

Another form of procrastination is trying to be too organized. Don't sit in your office, organizing your desk, and setting up the "perfect filing system" with typed labels and color-coded folders. Don't misunderstand; you need to be organized. One of the biggest reasons people are average in sales is that they "fly by the seat of their pants". They don't have a plan. Also, do your organization tasks at night and on the weekends. If you've learned as much as you can in training, and you are fairly organized, get out of the house and GO SEE CUSTOMERS.

Remember, your first six months of any new job are going to be tough. You are going to have to work extremely hard so don't expect to work from nine to five and then go out "partying" the rest of the night. Understand that your boss is expecting you to do all the great things you said you would and this will require extremely hard work during the first six months to a year. Those that consistently do well throughout their career continue to work hard, but maybe just not quite as hard as their first year. They have developed the ability to work much smarter than they did when they first got started. They now know all the customers and the products inside and out.

The second point to make is that if you are starting a new sales job or your company has realigned territories, you must immediately identify where you have existing business, in your new accounts, and get out and see those customers. The minute a company loses a sales rep or changes territories, your competition knows about it immediately. In fact, voice mails are probably traded back and forth throughout their company, giving intelligence reports about reps that leave, that move to new territories or that get promoted.

A great sales rep will get into the open territories or accounts and pounce on the business left vulnerable by someone leaving and you being in training. THEY DON'T PROCRASTINATE in going after your business. In fact, while in training, you or your manager should call each large customer and let them know that you are on board and will be out to see them soon. To that point, if you ever know of a competitive rep leaving their territory, you need to immediately get into their old accounts, where they had business, and start working on converting their business.

What many average reps will do, though, is to procrastinate getting into new accounts that have been assigned to them. Once they've spent the time getting to know their customers in their old territories and have gotten comfortable, they now view it as a "hassle" to go meet new customers, face possible rejection or hear stories about how great the last rep was.

Well, it always happens. Two months later they are under a major competitive threat and are thrown into a "flight of the bumblebee" trying to save the business. At this point they have no relationships with their new customers and basically everyone is thinking to themselves, "where have they been for the last two or three months?" "They don't deserve to keep the business". The next step is the rep begins asking the company to play a price game in order to save the business. They should have immediately gotten into the new accounts, establish relationships, re-sold the features and benefits of their great products, and built a quick fence around their business so they don't have to play the price game.

12 | KNOW YOUR CUSTOMER.

> *"There is only one boss. The customer. And he can fire every-
> body in the company from the chairman on down, simply by
> spending his money somewhere else.*
>
> SAM WALTON, FOUNDER, WAL-MART

How simple but true. Take the time to know and understand your customer. The customer is boss and the better you get at reading them, the better you will do at sales.

A lot of books have been written on this subject. To be a great sales rep, you need to learn how to "read" people. For those of you that this comes naturally, you may not be able to understand why it's so difficult. Believe me, there are many people who just have no natural ability when it comes to this. Thus, for those of you that fall into this category, you need to study and read about this fine art.

It's very painful to watch a sales rep who doesn't see the non-verbal and verbal clues that tell the real story. These clues might include the fact that someone doesn't like them or that they don't have time to talk. An observant rep can detect when a customer has no interest in what they are saying or who is uninterested in their product. The really good reps know how to pick up on these clues early, and to turn that knowledge to their advantage.

The first step in knowing a customer is to know and understand what "makes them tick"; to recognize the personality type they have. If you don't have this skill you must be open to coaching from your manager or you must learn about this skill set on your own. Let your manager help you develop this "sense of your customers" as I believe it can be developed in most people and it is key to being a top rep.

Watching people flounder in this area, is not only painful, it is

73

also frustrating and tiring. They are usually the ones that are poor performers and they often become incredibly defensive if you provide any sort of coaching or feedback as to ways that might help them improve their sales. Anything you suggest, they've "already done it" long before you suggest it. In other words, it's always the people who need it most who most strongly reject this kind of advice or coaching.

On the other hand, top reps are often open to any sort of suggestions that might give them one "gem", one idea, one tactic to increase their sales and get one "leg up" on the competition.

While there are some reps that seem to have been born with the talent to read people, not all of us were born with this trait. It is a skill that can be learned but you first must be open to learning. You must have an interest in understanding what motivates your customers. If you don't, you won't be very successful in sales. By understanding other people and their motivations, you will be more likely to say the right things and ask the right questions leading customers to buy your product. If you have a problem "reading" people, I highly suggest you read Ron Willingham's "Integrity Selling" as well as other books on the subject.

Keep in mind, Michael Jordon, Tiger Woods, Dan Marino, Muhammad Ali and Cal Ripken all had coaches. Can you imagine giving these guys suggestions as to how to improve their game? The fact is that as an outsider, or someone observing, a coach or manager can pick up little things that the sales rep, artist or athlete just doesn't see. The truly great ones are always working with coaches to better their performance. They're looking for that edge to be even better. They want to be the best and they don't mind hearing other's opinions.

So, open your mind and encourage your manager to give you ideas or suggestions. I don't believe Phil Jackson, the legendary coach of the Chicago Bulls and the L.A. Lakers, would claim to have had anywhere near the on-court skills of basketball player Michael Jordon during the time he coached Michael. But, Jackson is a great observer; a great strategist; a great idea man, and a great coach. You can be sure that Michael was open to most of his coach's suggestions. Michael knew that he was twice the ball player as Phil and as a result, he wasn't insecure of his ability, thus he had no reason to be defensive. I'm sure he didn't always agree with what coach had to say, but more times than not, Phil helped improve his game.

No great sales rep can make 100% of the people happy 100% of the time. No great rep is liked by every one of their customers, but they are liked by the majority of them. That's because they truly care about their customers. They are considerate. They take time to find out how their customers are doing in their lives and work, but they don't overstep the limits of the customer-sales rep relationship. You can usually tell the great reps, from the not-so-great reps simply by seeing who has the strongest relationships with their customers.

Everyone has a few impossible, difficult customers in their territory. These are the ones who eat their young and who everyone fears. The easy thing to do is avoid these people like the plague and average reps, who are easily intimidated, will do just that. Great reps will say, "I am going to win this woman or man over and they are going to love me". And you know what? The great ones do! The great ones figure out a way to make it happen.

Now, there are some great sales reps who aren't loved but they are respected. They succeed without becoming good friends with their customers. They earn respect with their honesty, hard work, follow-up, concern for their customer's time and needs, knowledge, expertise, and the value they bring to the table. Each of you will have your own strengths. This book merely points out those traits great reps possess and those things they do to be the best. That doesn't mean that they do all of them or that they possess every trait. But they do tend to possess many of them and they do most of the things necessary.

One of my sales reps claimed to have had 70% market share, which was incredibly high for our company. But even the best reps sometime miss signals from their customers. While she did have incredible relationships with many of her customers, as time went on it became obvious that some didn't care for her aggressive style. She described one in particular as "tough" and I'm sure he was. During the two separate sales calls I made with her, he seemed to be quite amenable, but I did notice that their personalities seemed to clash which wasn't obvious to her.

They were both "type A" overachievers. They both like to control conversations and you could see him getting annoyed with her. He stopped her on several occasions and said, "Now, look" and proceeded to correct her line of thinking. I'm not sure it occurred to her that he may not have particularly "felt comfortable" with her and I think she was intimidated by him. She thought he was "tough" but I believe it may have just been a clash of personalities.

While her personality seemed to work with many customers, it failed with others. If she would have worked to understand each customer's personality and motivations, she could have increased her market share even further. What is the best way to better understand customers? Do a lot more listening and a lot less talking. Due to her being uncomfortable with him, I found her to be doing a lot of talking. Had she asked some good questions, the outcome might have been different. Asking good open-ended questions shows you care about your customers and their needs.

The lesson here is that you must figure out each customer's personality type, tailor your discussions to them, pace the conversation, and ask the right questions for that customer. Customize the conversation to their personality, not yours. Talking too much and not reading customers are two of the biggest mechanical mistakes I see sales reps make and we are all guilty of this at one point or another.

13 | DETERMINE YOUR CUSTOMER'S NEEDS BY ASKING SOLID, OPEN-ENDED QUESTIONS.

Customer: I'd like some rat poison.
Clerk: Will you take it with you?
Customer: No, I'll send the rats over to get it.

JOEY BISHOP

Asking the right questions is so important that I want to devote a whole chapter to it.

The true essence of great salesmanship is to always ask solid, open-ended questions, while avoiding close-ended yes/no questions. You can't sell someone something they don't want or need. You can create the need and desire but you've got to do it by asking them the right questions. People don't always want a particular product, but they may want the things it brings them. If someone buys a Lexus or Mercedes it may be for the prestige it brings. The car itself may be secondary.

How will you know what a customer truly wants? You will know by asking them insightful questions. By knowing their wants and needs, you are then armed with the knowledge to be able to show how your product meets those needs.

Remember, if the customer asks you a question and you don't know the answer, let them know you will get the answer. If you tell someone you'll get them an answer, DO IT, and do it fast! Again, people buy from those that they like, they trust and those that do what they say.

It is often said that we were given two ears and one mouth, thus we should listen to customers twice as much as we talk. Volumes have been written about this. Great salespeople listen to what the customer needs and wants. They don't drone on and on about things that don't interest the customer. There's nothing that drives customers crazier than someone who doesn't stop talking; especially about things they don't care about.

I've already said that to be a top rep, you've got to be able to "read" your customers, and ask great questions. Now I will add one more thing: know when to shut up. I pull my hair out (and I don't have a lot of hair left), watching some reps "babble" on while the customer squirms in their chairs getting impatient or angry.

It seems as though some reps just don't get it. You've got to "tune in" to people. These are usually the same people who, in their personal lives, won't let you off the telephone. You give them every possible clue that you have to go and they just keep on talking until you finally have to just cut them off, raise your voice and say, "I gotta go". Remember, LISTEN TWICE AS MUCH AS YOU TALK. Keep yourself in check and in tune. Be a welcomed sales rep, not someone from whom people run and hide. Catch a clue and get tuned in!

Many sales reps avoid asking questions for two reasons:

1) They are afraid to lose control of the conversation.

2) They are afraid to look stupid.

As you go through sales training with your company, trainers will stand up in front of the classroom and go over slide after slide about the features and benefits of your products. Learn them all but once you get out into the field, don't data dump everything you have learned on the customer. Don't verbally vomit all over them. Find out what they're really thinking. Look for non-verbal clues as to your customer's mood.

You can always tell when you are doing a good job listening: when a customer tells you they only have a few minutes to spare, but an hour later you are still discussing your products. Ask good questions then use all that information in your head to ask them even more directed questions based on your knowledge. In the end, you'll close the sale, because you listened and you lead them to your product through planned questions.

I recently bought a truck from a dealer and was waiting in the lobby for them to get it ready. I struck up a conversation with the Sales Manager, about sales and his sales team. I asked him how he worked his way up to the top of the sales organization and he explained it was by being a top salesperson. I then asked him what differentiated him from the other sales people, and his answer, "I always sold the customer what they wanted; not what I wanted to sell them or what I thought they needed". Now, how do you think he found out what they wanted?..........He asked great questions.

By listening to your customers you can usually pick up on their signals that they are ready to buy. Once you pick up on these signals, you can use a "closing" question to make the sale. The worst thing in the sales world is to have convinced a customer to buy your product but not even realize it. Many reps will just keep on talking until they've finally said something that "undoes" the sale. They talk so much, that they finally plant a seed of doubt in the customers mind. DON'T OVERSELL A PRODUCT by continuing to talk when your customer is already sold on your product.

Always be looking for buying signals and try a few "trial closes" along the way. Again, by asking questions throughout a presentation, you can get buying signals from a customer. When you get the signal; if you sense they are ready, ask them for the business or ask them to take the next step necessary to get involved with your product. The next step might be an evaluation. Just be careful you don't oversell someone.

14 | TRULY CARE ABOUT YOUR CUSTOMERS.

A handyman's ad: "I can fix anything your husband can and I'll do it now".

In a recent study, by Harvard, they found that the number one trait of a great sales rep was that they cared more about the customer's situation than they cared about making the sale. I have personally seen great sales reps recommend a competitor's product because in their mind they knew it would be better for the patient and the doctor. That sort of gesture, once in a while, will entrust you to your customer. Just don't use it too often!

Maybe the best example of "putting the customer first" comes from Johnson & Johnson. In the early 1980s, someone put cyanide in bottles of Tylenol, the number one pain reliever in the world. The executives of Johnson and Johnson could have just waited it out, to see if any more appeared, but they chose to do what was right for the customers.

The top executives met in the corporate meeting rooms and discussed the possible remedies. Should they just recall certain lot numbers? Should they only recall product in that area of the country? Should they do nothing? There could be only one answer. After reviewing the J&J Credo they realized they must put the safety of the customers first, regardless of cost. The only thing to do was to recall every single bottle of Tylenol around the world. It cost J&J millions, but today Tylenol is still the number one pain reliever because they did what was best for the customer.

15 | BECOME A PART OF THE CUSTOMER'S TEAM

"But we often look so long and so regretfully upon the closed door that we do not see the one which has opened for us."

HELEN KELLER

Every day in our selling career, we need to keep the customer's best interest at heart. If we do our customers will trust us and give us more of their business.

The Harvard Study, mentioned in the last chapter, found that customers, who are treated right, begin to trust sales people so much that they actually become a part of their team. Rather than being just another sales rep, one of many calling on that customer, a good salesperson can become an adviser, consultant, and friend. Once you reach this level, it becomes very hard for you to lose business because your customers have so much trust in you and you bring so much value to them.

A professional relationship with a customer can entail a lot of different things. I know a few reps that are successful without doing things outside of work with their customers but not many. If you truly love sales; truly love and care about your customers; get to know them outside the work environment. You can be successful even if you don't do this, but it's harder and it takes a lot longer.

When you are in your customer's office, they are often under pressure; they don't have a lot of time; they've got work to get done or they've got patients who need attending. Out on the golf course, tennis court, at dinner or anywhere away from work, they can truly get to know you as a person, not just as a sales rep, and just as important, you can get to know them.

I realize that for some of you, expense budgets may be a con-

---

81

cern. Get creative. Share the expense with other, non-competitive reps. You don't have to take them to a $200 dinner. Go grab a $15 lunch. Go jogging with them. If you find out their interests, they are often economical and the customers might love you to join them. I had one rep who found out his customer liked tour bike racing. He joined him several weekends, on training runs, and they became fast friends. He started getting business from him very quickly.

So, if you are truly dedicated to becoming a top sales rep, make your relationships and friendships as strong as possible with your customers. Become a part of their team by going the extra mile, which most reps just won't do.

One of the best reps who ever worked for me, Tom Worthington, goes bow hunting and fly-fishing with various customers. And they each pay their own way! Competitive companies were constantly sending new sales reps in to do battle with Tom and they just kept quitting. Tom takes a sincere interest in his customers and enjoys their friendship. But Tom wasn't a top sales rep just because he became friends with his customers. He also did the other things listed in this book. Recently, Tom was promoted after turning down five or six previous offers to be promoted in the past. He loves sales and his customers so much he found it hard to walk away. They finally made him an offer he couldn't refuse but he is helping reps throughout the country with his expertise and knowledge.

When I first started in medical sales, I was asked to help sponsor a charity golf tournament for the local chapter of the AORN (Association of Operating Room Nurses). There's nothing like operating room nurses. They are in a class of their own. They are very fun, caring people that take their jobs and the care of their patients very seriously.

So, here I come rolling into the parking lot, in my company issued Ford Taurus, and out of the corner of my eyes I see a crowd of people huddled around a beautiful Range Rover. Taking a closer look, I realized it's many of my new customers, BarBQ-ing and tail gaiting out of the back of one of my biggest competitor's truck. I had seen this guy about a month before, yelling, screaming, and having fun at another event, kidding around with everyone. My heart sunk. How was I ever going to compete with this charismatic son-of-a–gun. As I rounded the corner, I could see him waving his spatula at me just rubbin' it in.

Well, the happy ending of the story is that I developed my own relationships and friendships with these same customers, and I became very successful in that territory. I actually became good friends with this guy and our two companies started working together on a large, mutual contract we were awarded.

That said, make sure you are true to yourself. Don't try to be someone you're not. People will like you for who you are and the minute you try to fake it, they'll see right through you. As for my friendly competitor, I will never be like him, and he will never be like me. He always gave me a hard time about my image, my suits, button down shirts, and my "corporate policy". But I'd just smile because for me it worked and for him, his looser style was just as effective.

As you begin your journey to build relationships, working to become part of the customer's team, it will be difficult at first. When you take over new accounts, you may get beaten up pretty badly. They may spend your entire first visit telling you how great the last sales rep was and how much they loved them. On the other side of the coin, they may tell you how much they disliked the last rep and how much they dislike your company and its products. It can be pretty depressing if you don't prepare yourself mentally.

What you've got to do is to remind yourself, before every call, that you are a great sales rep and you will win them over. Then you need to set out to provide value, build a friendship, and always do what you say you'll do. The last thing you want to do is let customers see "dollar signs" in your eyes. If they believe all you care about is selling them something, and you don't care about them as people, you'll never sell them a thing.

As your partnerships, relationships and friendships grow, there will come a day when you can arrive at an account, unannounced, not check into material management, get into the locker room, because they gave you the code, and stroll into the back, with the rest of the staff. That's the day when you know you have arrived as a valued member of their team. They don't view you anymore, merely as a sales rep, but as an integral part of their team.

16 TREAT EVERYONE WITH RESPECT; BE HONEST; AND GAIN THEIR TRUST

"ANYONE CAN BE POLITE TO A KING, BUT IT TAKES A GENTLEMEN TO BE POLITE TO A BEGGAR."

JIM SHEA

Treating people with respect is not only important in life, but it is also critical to your sales career. Early in my life, I was taught to be respectful of all people, regardless as to their job, economic status, sex, religion or race. My parents were strict about being polite, honest, ethical, moral and unprejudiced. It was just not acceptable for me, or my siblings, to not say thank you when someone did something for us. If we got caught in a lie, there was hell to pay.

As I got older, I realized that by being nice, friendly, and respectful to people of all backgrounds and at all levels of economic and job status, it greatly benefited my sales career and more importantly my soul. Many medical sales reps would focus almost entirely on the surgeons, often ignoring the scrub techs, nurses, and orderlies in the operating room. This technique might work in the short term, but people remember the reps who ignore and "snub" them. Once your products have competition, the people that you ignored will go out of their way to get back at you.

Take orderlies, for example. These are basically people who clean up the operating rooms. Technically, they're not even part of the clinical support team. As a sales person, you wouldn't think there is a sales reason to talk to them or be nice to them; other than just being a nice human being. But over the years, I've found that orderlies can be a great source of information in the hospital. They know which doctors are in a good mood and which ones to avoid. They know the politics of the place. And they are privy to the competition's products and sales efforts.

So, unlike some sales reps, I made it a point to be nice to everyone I met in the accounts, and I reaped the rewards. You just never know where you are going to get information that can be useful and this applies to any industry. It's not only right to be nice to those lower on the totem pole for your sales, but it's the right thing to do as a human being.

Many sales books stress that you should not waste time selling to people that don't have the authority to make a decision. That is true for the most part and up to a point. You must be careful, though, because in many industries, people at different levels can have an influence on the decision makers as to which products are bought and used.

To repeat: Treating everyone with respect, and viewing everyone as a source of information or as someone who might be able to help, can be among a sales person's greatest tools. This is true no matter what you sell whether you are selling surgical equipment, business forms, or insurance.

Relationships are key. You don't have to be the funniest rep in the world or the one that everyone gathers around at the party. Just be a good person, take an interest in people, be consistent, be a good listener and always do what you say you will do. This is so important. If you tell someone you only need 15 minutes of their time, then when those 15 minutes are up, you need to stand up and tell them, "my 15 minutes are up and I don't want to overstay my welcome". If the customer has more time, they will let you know. By sticking to what you tell people, you will always be welcomed back.

On your way to becoming a top sales rep, be sure to read Harvey MacKay's *How to Swim with the Sharks and Not Get Eaten Alive.* He provides 66 great questions to ask your key customers. They include questions about their interests, where they went to college, etc., which show that you have a true interest in them. Furthermore, this knowledge can also provide topics of future discussion and ways that you can continually show them you care about them as people.

As I discussed in an earlier chapter, another way to show respect for your customers and to gain their trust is to always be honest. Just remember, if they catch you being dishonest, it will be "sales death". They will never fully trust you again.

You can also gain trust by being up front with your customers when things go wrong. If your company has backorders, let the customer know before they run out of product. Give them the opportunity to plan ahead. This will build your relationship with them, their trust, and their confidence in you as a person and as a rep.

Remember, "Under promise and over deliver". Don't ever tell them a problem will be fixed in two weeks, when you know it will be at least four. If you tell them it will be four and it only turns out to be two, you are a hero and they will always trust your word and the information you provide. Tell them two weeks and it takes four and they will never believe anything you tell them.

Honesty is still and will always be the best policy. If you are a dishonest person, people will figure you out eventually. You may make the sale in the short run, but in the long run, you will have to move on and find a new job because people will quit buying from you.

Honesty, integrity and maintaining a high moral and ethical standard are not only important with your customers, but they are important with your co-workers, your family, friends and anyone you know or meet. I definitely believe in Karma or Synchronicity; whatever you want to call it. If you put out negative "vibes" you will get negative "vibes" or energy back. Put out positive energy and your life will be enriched.

When other reps are sitting around complaining and being negative; run as fast as you can. Sometimes, there are circumstances in which things are unfair, and the entire sales force is up in arms, but usually those sitting around gossiping and complaining about every little thing are the losers. Be very careful not to get caught up in gossip because many times the rumors are untrue and outright lies. If you spread gossip about people, very bad things will come to your life. I have seen it time and time again.

As I reflect back through my life and career, I realize that all those people who gossiped and tried to cause harm to others, it seems as though terrible things eventually came to them. I'm not kidding about this stuff. I saw many people eventually get fired and their reputations were ruined or scarred because they lied about others or were unfair to people.

Once, an incompetent president I knew was firing people left and right, hurting people's careers, due to his dishonesty, lack of ethics and leadership abilities. He was dishonest to himself and the company, and was trying to hide his secret by hiding behind others. I saw him fire one Vice President who knew more in his right "pinky" about their business then the President would ever understand. The VP had been a loyal employee with the company for many years, having been very successful in one of their non-US Divisions. They promoted him to run a very important segment of their business in the U.S but due to the President's incompetence, that segment began to fail and he fired the long-term loyal employee. Eventually, the very bright CEO of the company realized what was happening and he fired the President. So, eventually, truth and justice prevails. So stay truthful and don't run others down, through gossip and lies, due to your own insecurities.

Don't be like this. Stand up and do the right things. Stand up and be honest and ethical, every day of your life. Don't lie about people. People will respect you more and you will get them to stand behind you through "thick and thin". They will help you out tremendously during your career. Isn't it amazing that we were only given 10 main, basic commandments, and so many people have such a hard time with "Thou shall not bare false witness against thy neighbor"? It seems as though it always comes back to haunt and hurt those unethical people, one way or another. So don't let it happen to you.

I had one rep who made it a point to constantly gossip and make things up about his co-workers. Eventually, no one liked him within the company, and the people inside the corporate office dragged their feet to help him. You could tell he was a very bitter person and that he was very troubled in his personal life. Stay on the "up and up" and you will be fine. It is good for your "Karma" and good for your mental state of mind. Your life will be much happier when you work in harmony with those around you. When your life is in better harmony, you will sell more products. See how it's all tied together?

Always remember who your "customer" is at that given moment. At one point, you may have called on people who don't even use your product but are buyers. As you change or move up in sales, to more technical or expensive products, your customers may change and you may call on those who actually use your product. If your product is more technical, or less of a commodity, the end-user, such as a physician or engineer may drive the sale more than anyone else.

In most industries, the more technical or expensive a product, the higher up the chain-of-command the decision must go. As your career changes or as you are promoted, you may be selling products that can greatly impact the bottom line of the company. The person making the ultimate decision may be the CEO, CFO, physician, architect or chief engineer.

But, as you get accustomed to working with higher levels in the organization, you must avoid a few common mistakes. First, don't forget the people who helped get you there, the "little guys" who bought your products in the past. If you do, they will remember it when they rise up in the organization.

Second, even if a senior-level person is making the final decision, don't forget the department supervisor. He or she may still have influence, and if they think you are going around them, they'll find a way to keep your product off the shelves.

In other words, as you begin to call on people, higher up in an organization, you may think you no longer need to deal with people "lower on the food chain". But these people can make your life miserable and they still may have enough control to block you accomplishing your sales goal. If they don't now, they might in the future. Understand that every situation is different, but keep your eyes, ears, and mind open to the proper way to work each account. The problem with some reps is they decide there is a certain way to do business and that's the way they are going to do it.

Some managers may tell you that the only person you should be calling on is the CFO of every account. Now, in general, he may be correct in that 85% of the time, the CFO is going to make the decision, but in many organizations, the financial administrators, accountants, or others may have a strong influence on the CFO. Ignore them and you could be done. Look at Donald Trump's "The Apprentice" Show? He always had his two advisors giving him feedback. He made the decision, but he listened to them and they had an influence on him. Just be flexible and analyze each situation. Don't get so rigid you miss the boat.

The longer you stay in an industry and your success level increases, you'll have strong personal relationships with many of your customers. What may happen is you'll begin to lose patience with people that try to block you in getting to those "friends". You've got to be careful. You have got to keep playing the game, because sometimes those "road blockers" still have the power to stop you if they think you are not respecting them or their position of power. Even if you manage to get in through the back door, through your friends, the "road blocker" will continue to work to get you and your products thrown out of the account in long run term.

Great reps know there is an art to "walking this line". Sometimes you'll have to do what you have to do, to get your product into the account, and that may mean by-passing those road blockers but somehow you'll have to make those "road blockers" feel they were part of the process.

17 | RELAX AND HAVE FUN WITH YOUR JOB AND CUSTOMERS

"If the fans don't want to come to the stadium, there's no way you can stop them."

THE GREAT YOGI BERRA

I'm not sure I know what Yogi meant, but you have to have fun with your job and you've got to be "yourself" when calling on customers. Relax. You can't force the situation, just like you can't force fans to come to the stadium. Always do the best you can. Know your material, believe in your product, ask great questions, have written goals, be fully prepared, but once you are in front of the customer, be yourself. That's all you can do. If you take that attitude, people will sense your confidence and they will enjoy being around you. It always seems as though the best reps just seem to be enjoying life and having fun. When they are having fun, customers are having fun. So be yourself and keep it light. Don't take yourself too seriously. It's boring.

Even the best reps, though, sometimes get nervous on big sales calls, but they find a way to hide their fear. Life's too short. Sales should be fun. What better job is there than to ride around and meet with people all day, learn more about customers and their needs, and get them to use your products that fill those needs; all the while making money doing it? Accept the fact that there will be some customers who are rude and don't appreciate you. Don't let it get you down. Stay positive and keep having fun!

I don't want anyone to think sales is an easy job. I have probably worked harder in sales than I ever did in any other vocation. There is pressure and you must be able to accept rejection, but at the same time, sales has been the most rewarding and enjoyable job I've ever had.

It is just inevitable that you will run into some tough customers. It is also inevitable that you will run into setbacks with your job and with your life, for that matter. Life will never be a totally smooth ride. Just think of the setbacks as opportunities for you to learn. You can get so focused on your goals that when you hit the setbacks or roadblocks, you "over focus" which can cause you to make mistakes. You may get impatient and make bad moves in your investments, or the way you handle your customers. When the tough times arrive, be sure to stay calm and work towards enjoying life.

There have been times, when I have been so focused on my goals, that when I hit setbacks, I am miserable. It affected every aspect of my life and in the end, it just wasn't productive and it wasn't worth it. If you are unhappy, because you put so much pressure on yourself, then what's the sense of doing it all? Someone once said, "Happiness is not a destination, but rather the journey".

So, do all the things I discuss in this book, but realize that even the best sales reps in the world, experience set backs. Don't force the situation and don't drive yourself crazy. Stay calm, keep working hard, brainstorm with friends and associates, and you will make it through. Enjoy the ride along the way, regardless of the terrain.

I had another great sales rep that worked for me, Ben Alfelor, who never seemed to have a bad day. He was always upbeat, laughing, and having fun. Even when the customers were giving him problems, you never knew it with Ben. When the customers were around Ben, they couldn't help but laugh and have fun as well. He's just a great guy and has succeeded incredibly in sales. He also won Sales Rep of the Year at J&J's ETHICON Endosurgery, which, to me, winning Sales Rep of the Year at any company is like winning the Super Bowl of sales. It is something that very few people achieve.

A few years ago, I worked with a sales rep who had been around a while. His two kids were almost out of school, he had a wonderful wife, and he owned a beautiful home. He should be been at the top of his game. He should have been having fun. Instead, he was a mess in front of his customers. He was smacking his gum nervously and couldn't focus on the job at hand. Instead of asking good questions and customizing the calls to his customers, he was fumbling through his product samples and losing his audience quickly. One customer, a jokester, sensed his nervousness and just drilled this guy every which way he could. He seemed to enjoy watching him squirm. Had he just relaxed, laughed, asked a few good questions, instead of trying to "data dump", he would have taken back control of the call.

The problem is that as sales reps get more experienced, they can get sloppy. They think they are too good for refresher courses in basic sales. They have a little money in the bank and they just don't care anymore.

When times get tough, and they do for the best of us, it is important to remember what got you to the top in the past. Maybe it was your ability to work with all types of people at different levels. It was probably your ability to adjust to every situation, to anticipate tough customers and not back them into a corner. No sales rep can be loved by all their customers, but if you come prepared and organized, and remember to have fun, you can win most of the people over most of the time.

Every territory will have one or two customers who love to be the "intimidators". They get enjoyment out of getting under people's skin. Accept the fact that you will have to deal with customers like this sooner or later. Rather than get intimidated, just make the decision now to find a way to win them over. You are going to go the extra mile. You are going to figure out what makes them tick. Remind yourself that no one is better than you. No matter what these people say to you or how they act, you are going to stay calm and composed.

BE A BRIGHT SPOT IN SOMEONE'S DAY

You might not be the most exciting person in the world but that doesn't mean you have to stay that way. Remember my recommendation that people read for at least fifteen minutes each day to improve their sales ability? The same thing applies to improving other facets of your life. If you struggle to make conversation with people or you believe you are boring, start reading every book on the subject of conversation. An all-time classic is "How to Win Friends and Influence People" by Dale Carnegie. Every sales rep should read that book, regardless as to whether you have a great personality or not.

If you take a sincere interest in others and ask questions about what interests them, they will turn a two-minute call into a twenty-minute call; and you'll always be welcomed back. Talk about things they're not interested in, and they will always be busy when you call for an appointment.

Try to be different than all the other reps in everything you do. For instance, most reps bring in donuts or bagels when they spend the day in an account. That's pretty boring! Almost every rep brings in donuts or bagels. Why not do something different so people not only remember you, they look forward to your next visit? Dare to be different in everything you do.

One rep, with whom I worked, would set up table-top-displays and would give prizes to customers that answered questions correctly, after her in-service. Sure, any rep can hand out pens, pads, key chains and other promotional items, but why not think of a fun way to make customers work for them and learn something in the process. She would set up the game "Operation" and if they could remove the "bone" without the buzzer sounding, they could go on to a bonus question for another prize. The customers loved it and they loved her.

18 | DEMONSTRATE YOUR PRODUCT; DON'T JUST TALK ABOUT IT

Asking lots of good, open-ended questions will only get you so far. Eventually, you will need to do some well-thought out, clever product demonstrations or presentations. If possible, you should do everything you can to get your customers involved with those demos. You need to get their hands on the product.

Many reps are lousy at giving product demonstrations. They just talk, talk, talk, talk, talk; putting everyone to sleep, expounding on their thoughts about the world and their products. This is the wrong approach. Rather than talk, you should start your demonstration the same way you begin other steps of the sale: ask good questions. As you demonstrate, continue asking good questions. Make sure you are still focusing in on what interests the customer so you lead them to buy your product. People don't want you to tell them a product is good for them. They want to decide that for themselves. You can get them to feel good about your product by showing them in a demonstration how the product will meet their needs. Also, getting them involved with the demo always helps.

Study after study shows that people only retain 20% of what they hear but if they hear and see something, it shoots up to 60%. The more senses you can bring into a sales call the greater the chance you will sell the product. Your company spends tens of thousands of dollars, sometimes more, creating impressive brochures and demonstration kits to show your products in the best light. Companies wouldn't do this if it didn't help sales reps sell more products; so make sure you utilize them.

I wish I could tell you that all these suggestions are mine – but they're not. I learned almost every one of them from watching successful sales reps, managing over 80 reps, and from former managers (who were also successful sales reps at one time). I also learned by watching my competition; the things they did right and the things they did wrong. Other great sources of ideas were sales books. And finally, I learned through direct experience, with trial and error, in my own sales career.

19 | DON'T PLAY THE PRICE GAME IF YOU WANT TO BE ON TOP

"Sell on price, lose on price."

Over the long term, you can't win by selling on price alone. Your competitors will just lower their price, and you'll get caught in a downward spiral. Your company won't tolerate it and they won't be able to remain profitable. Sometimes, however, if you lower your price far enough, material managers or buyers will force the issue and insist end-users to try the product. Usually, your gain from this tactic will be short lived. The end users will resent the fact that they were forced to use what they perceived to be an inferior product, and they will work to do whatever it takes to get your product thrown out.

That's not to say that your product is inferior, but when you sell on price, that is the perception. Any little thing that goes wrong will be quickly brought to the attention of EVERYONE. One thing is certain: *playing the price game is a fast way to run a company and your career into the ground.* A company must be profitable in the long run and selling on price is counter-productive to those efforts.

If you lead with price, your customers will never remain loyal, and they will switch the first time someone else comes along with a lower price. It is not only a destructive approach for you, but for your industry as well. When playing pick up baseball, have you ever "climbed" the bat to see who bats first? Someone eventually wins or loses because there is no more room left on the bat.

It's the same with pricing. If you sell on price, your competitor will respond with a lower price. Eventually there is no more "price" to give and no more profit to be had. Usually, the company left holding the bat now has their products selling at an unprofitable price;

which will quickly lead to failure. Sell on price and you and your company will lose on price.

The great companies aren't always the most expensive but they certainly aren't the cheapest. They make higher quality products that add value for customers, and great salespeople are able to demonstrate that value to the customer. Some material managers "trip over quarters to get to pennies" but savvy economic buyers take an interest in understanding the differences between the products they buy. They consider the value of a product, not just the price.

A great example, in the medical industry, is when hospitals buy the cheapest surgical or medical gloves. Every day, people are ripping and tearing glove after glove when using the cheap ones. Over time, the hospital ends up spending much more for their gloves than if they had gone with the slightly more expensive glove. Great reps take the time to present cost analysis to educate customers about the value of their products. How many times in your personal lives have you bought cheap only to regret it later? The first thing you think in your mind, when the cheap product falls apart is, "I should have paid a little more". Well, it's amazing how many people forget this lesson in their professional lives. Make sure you remind them and sell the value and benefits of your products.

A sure sign of an average rep is the guy who constantly calls his manager asking for the lowest allowable pricing in order to gain new business. The great reps spend time "selling" the benefits of the product to the end user. Price is the last topic of discussion. Many times, if the customer sees no value in your product in the first place, they won't buy it, no matter how cheap. Great sales reps, sell the product based on value. "Order takers" sell on *price*. If all your customer cares about is price, be prepared to walk away from the business.

You rarely see a top sales representative with the lowest average selling prices (ASP's), in their territory, compared to other reps and territories. The only time you might see this occur is when the top rep has penetrated their accounts so deep and has such high market share, that the customers have earned the lowest price levels, through volume discounts from your company. Even then, top reps find a way to keep their ASP's high because they are constantly selling value, not price.

The standard response to competitive pressure, from average reps, is to run to their company and request a price decrease, without getting all the facts and understanding the true situation in the account. Many times buyers or material managers will call you into their office and threaten to switch the business unless you lower your price. If you have entrenched yourself and your product, in the minds of the end-users, many times it will be impossible for the material managers to make good on that threat.

That doesn't mean that there aren't situations in which you may have to lower your price. But even as you do so, make sure you are constantly re-selling the features and benefits of your products. Whenever you have a competitive threat, you must fight the battles, and that might include taking a look at your pricing. But there are other tools in your box as well.

Great reps are constantly bringing their customers new clinical or technological information, new ways for them to enhance their business, and other value added benefits. By selling value, you will help educate your customers and help them avoid the same mistake of "tripping over quarters, in order to go after pennies". I see so many buyers doing this, I just have to laugh and shake my head. If you educate your customers, you can help them avoid making this foolish mistake.

20 | ASK FOR THE ORDER. CLOSE THE BUSINESS

"Rhinoceroses charge with singleness of purpose. All of your energies are directed toward the attainment of your one burning desire."

SCOTT ALEXANDER,
AUTHOR OF RHINOCEROS SUCCESS

To be a top sales rep, you must ask for the order. You must close business. A top sales rep, in Scott Alexander's words, is "A Rhinoceros, one that keeps charging ahead". You must have written goals, back them by a burning desire and then charge forward until you obtain the orders allowing you to achieve those goals. As a sales rep, you must close the sale.

This is one of the most important points in becoming a successful sales rep. I can't tell you how many reps I've worked with who had most of the things they needed to be successful; great relationships, great product knowledge, and a strong work ethic. The problem was they would never ask for the business. This is a fast track to failure. You've got to ask for the order. *Closing the business is the acid test of selling.* As long as you are a salesperson, your success and how you will be judged will be determined almost entirely by your ability to sell products and close business. Commissions, recognition, promotions, and sales awards basically come from your ability to close business.

No matter how knowledgeable you are, if you lead the customer 99% of the way, to buying your product, but you don't ask for the business, you've failed. If they don't actually give you an order, bringing the product onto their shelf, you haven't succeeded. You haven't sold anything until it's on their shelf; and that doesn't mean you've merely gotten them to allow you to consign the product on their shelves. That is one step in the sales process, but until they are using your product on a regular basis, you haven't sold them anything.

Too many times, customers promise to place orders, only to back out in the end. Often they may just tell you they will order your product because a powerful person asked them to. They tell you that merely to get rid of you and after you leave they conveniently forget. You check the system a few days later only to find the order was never placed. Now you have a problem, because if this person really doesn't want to place the order, they may try and block you from coming back.

Making customers feel good is a part of your job, but if you were hired merely to provide a good warm fuzzy feeling about your company and yourself, your title would be "public relations specialist". No, you were hired to sell product and it's no secret to your customers. When you go to visit them, they know why you are there. So, why do so many reps merely "drop" by to say hello and bring bagels? These types of reps just never achieve great success.

When a sales rep merely comes by to say hello and brings no value to the customers, the customers eventually won't see them anymore. I was speaking to a recruit I was considering hiring, and he said, "I like to be profit to my customers, rather than overhead". When you find a customer's needs; you present a product that fits that need; and it helps them in their business, that's being a "profit" to them. When you merely "stop by" and take up valuable time, you've become overhead.

Remember, you can do everything right on a sales call and get 99% of the way there, but if you don't get the order you have failed. You've failed yourself, your family, and your company. If you have a product that can truly meet the needs of a customer, you have failed them as well.

Great presentations don't put commission in your pocket; getting orders does.

Promises don't either. A customer telling you they'll place an order or buy from you at some future date, does nothing. People change their minds or turn to other vendors. They might go out of business or retire. One signed order is worth more than 100 promises to order.

Some of you may work incredibly hard to be the best at knowing clinical or technical data or knowing every feature and benefit of the product. Others may work hard at relationships, taking people to dinner and golf on the weekends. But if you never ask for the business or ask for the order, what good is all the rest?

You don't want to always have $$ signs in your eyes when you meet with customers. A great sales rep truly cares about his or her customer's well being and their needs, but that same rep is always thinking about closing the sale. You owe it to the customer that if you truly believe in the features, benefits and value of your products, to get them using the products.

The ultimate goal is to get the purchase order from your customer the first day you are face-to-face, but that isn't always possible. What you should strive towards is getting better and better at closing your sales, tightening up your presentations. If you are a weak closer, you will limit your income and success. Imagine if you work towards bettering your closing skills and can reduce the number of calls it takes you to close, from four calls to two. You cut your closing time in half and double your sales. You have now doubled the time you can now use to call on other customers.

Thinking about closing the sale needs to become second nature to you. Before you even set foot into an account, you need to have a goal in mind. You need to think about what you need to say or do in order to get a sale. If it is a longer sales cycle, figure out what you need to say or do to move the process along to the next step.

The ability to close sets great sales reps apart from the merely average or below-average sales person. Average people go through all the motions but never ask for the business. They believe that if they just drop in and pay a social visit, strengthening their relationships, that people will just naturally buy from them. Well, it's just not the case. Granted, people do tend to buy from people they like, so you must develop friendships and strong relationships. But it still comes down to asking for the business. What gives great reps the courage to ask for business? The burning desire to succeed.

Friendship is no guarantee that you'll close the sale. You're not the only sales rep the customer likes, so if they are buying from someone else they like, they'll just learn to like you but never buy from you. You've got to ASK FOR THE BUSINESS.

"Closing the sale" may mean different things at different times. Sometimes, your initial goal may be to get your product evaluated. You must plan your call and presentation so that you can lead the customer to be willing to evaluate your product. You must ask for the evaluation, just like you would ask for an order. After you get agreement to evaluate your product, you must agree upon acceptable outcomes of that evaluation that will lead to them buying your product.

For instance, if your product requires that 50 people evaluate it and provide feedback, it would be unacceptable, from your point of view, if it required 100% of those 50 people to approve the product. So, prior to the evaluation, you must set parameters with the buyer, director, or whoever has the final say, as to what those reasonable levels of acceptance are. Shoot low, like 60%. You might ask, "If 60% of the end-users like the product, can we bring it in for their use?" If they raise the level to 70%, you're golden. It's a lot better than 100%. Don't leave any loose ends. In other words, "closing the sale" in this instance means getting the customer to agree to evaluate your product, and if it meets his needs, then he will buy it.

And finally, if you close business on a call, why pack up and leave? If they bought from you at that moment, they probably like you; feel comfortable doing business with you; and they are in a buying mode. They may have time to hear about other products, whereas in a week or two, or on your next call, they may not. Don't forget the ole "by the way technique". As you're packing up, you might pause and say, "oh, by the way, have you seen the new product we just introduced last week?" as you pull out a brochure. They'll let you know in a subtle way if they have time to look. If they don't, move on to the next call. Many times, they will have the time and you can just tack on another product to the PO they just gave you.

21 | YOU'VE GOT TO ENTRENCH AND EXPAND THE USE OF YOUR PRODUCT

"A strong passion for any object will ensure success, for the desire of the end will point out the means."

WILLIAM HAZLITT

One of the worst mistakes a sales rep can make, is to take an order for a product, call it in, and then move on to the next customer. I've seen it happen time and time again. A few weeks later the rep finds the "ship sinking" and everything unraveling. It is inevitable that problems will arise after a conversion. Customers forget they agreed to switch, orders don't come in, the product codes in the computers don't get switched and on and on. Sometimes, customers will call your customer service and cancel the order they just gave you. You may get the order from the department that uses your product, but once the material manager finds out about it, he may "nix" the order due to "conflicting" contracts, etc. You cannot assume anything in the world of sales.

This means you must follow through on every sale you make and avoid moving on to the next sale until you have ensured success. What happens if your warehouse ships the wrong order of products? It might arrive at the receiving docs and be rejected because the products aren't listed on the PO. If you don't follow through, it could be several weeks before you even realize that they never got your product. By that time, your competitor could have gotten into the account because their friends tipped them off. Now they've "fixed" the problem, shutting you out.

You must pay special attention to the new customers until you are totally and 100% confident that everyone has settled in comfortably to using your product. Don't assume anything. Sometimes customers will tell you everything is fine and you let your guard down. Don't slip into this trap.

A "sale" really doesn't occur until (1) the product is on the shelf and (2) the customer is using it!

Another step in this follow-up process is to be sure to in-service the staff on all the shifts as to the use of your product. If you trained them before the sale, train them again. If someone misuses your product, because you assumed they were ready, you may find yourself losing the sale. You've also got to make sure your product is properly labeled on the shelf and that it is stocked in each room. You've got to be there, when that last difficult customer tries your product for the first time.

Never forget that in residual sales, the sale is never complete or over. In the long term, once a conversion takes place, your product is now on the shelf, and the customer is actually using your product, you still can never stop selling and reinforcing the benefits of your products to them. Why? Every day, your competitors are calling on your customers and giving them information to dispute your claims. They are constantly detailing their products to them and over time, your great sales presentations begin to fade and they forget how good looking you are.

You must set your customers on a periodic call pattern and plan to re-inservice or resell them on the benefits of your products on a consistent basis. You must constantly bring them articles, information, and data to substantiate your product. Gaining back lost customers is usually much more difficult then gaining new customers. Never take your customers for granted.

One of the best sales reps who ever worked for me, Bryan Abe, told me that he re-inservices or re-sells his customers a minimum of five times throughout a year. Bryan maintains about 85% market share and it's because he always does the things top sales reps do. Reinforcing his products, in the minds of his customers, is at the top of the list. His customers respect him and his knowledge at a level unmatched by other reps.

Walking away from existing customers not only threatens your existing business, but it eliminates one of the easiest ways to expand and grow your business. Once you have a satisfied customer, it is much easier to increase their use of your product, or get them to buy new products than it is to find new customers that know nothing about you or your products. Similarly, by asking them a few pointed questions, you can encourage customers to expand their use of your product beyond its original application, which means they will need more of it!

For instance, you might have sold a surgeon on using your surgical instrument for laparoscopic bowel resection; one of its common uses. But somewhere you learned that a few doctors are now using it for hernia repairs. The next month you stop by to check in on how things are going you should strike up a discussion with your new customer about this new application.

"Doctor, what sort of instrumentation do you currently use for your hernia repairs and what benefits do you get from those instruments?" Bingo! You've now got him/her giving you lots of valuable information. After you actively LISTEN to what he or she is telling you, you follow up with a question like, "Well, what would you think about an instrument that would provide those same benefits as what you are currently using, but also gives you the flexibility of x, y, or z?" You might explain that several doctors around the country have found that the very instrument he/she is using for bowel resection is working beautifully for hernia repairs. The connection is made and you get them to commit to trying it on their next case, which, of course you attend.

This brings up another important issue. *Any time a customer uses one of your products for the first time, you must be there, even if your customer doesn't see the need.* There are several reasons for this. First, your competitor may just show up during that first trial and plant seeds of doubt. Second, no matter how similar your product is to what they were using, there will be differences. If they get confused, they may just throw it across the room, unwilling to ever try it again. Third, it gives you the chance to have more exposure to the staff to build relationships. Finally, being there allows you to reinforce the benefits of your product as they are using it. What might seem to be an obvious benefit to you, because of your extensive training on the product, a customer might miss. Sometimes you have to point out benefits that may not always be obvious unless someone is looking for them.

Another common mistake sales reps make is to trade old business for new business. Don't work for months to close an account, get the business and the product stocked on the shelf and then walk away to go get new business. *Remember, when you sell in an industry of repeat business, you should never stop "selling" them on your products. You've got to constantly remind them as to why they bought your product in the first place.* The minute you stop, you can bet your competition is right behind you telling them all sorts of stories as to why your product is horrible and why they should be using their product.

Here's a message I sent to one of my sales teams that stresses the importance of keeping your eye on existing customers:

"One month does not make a trend, but when a customer is "plugging" along using three to four products per month, it should raise an alarm when one month has zero used. Please use these reports to manage your business. They are excellent and if you catch a competitive threat early on, there is still hope that you can reverse it. Once they settle in with the competition, they change preference cards, and a certain amount of time passes without problems, your chances of switching them back is slim and none, and "Slim may have already left town".

If you notice a downtrend in your reports, that customer may very well be in the throws of an evaluation, which gives you plenty of time to get in there, plant the seeds of doubt and combat the threat. Assume it's nothing; assume it's because of the slower months; assume it will just take care of itself and go away; assume the customer was on vacation; assume...assume....assume and the next thing you know, you've lost your business. Many times there is something else underlying, which causes you to lose the business, such as lack of account coverage, and they'll harbor ill feelings at you for a long time.

Hence, I strongly suggest that you take a good look at this report, and immediately get into these accounts and find out what's going on. We work much too hard to gain new business, to let lost business negate the gains. If you don't fight the battles and competitive threats, eventually you will run out of new customers to convert."

22 | DON'T LET OTHERS PULL YOU DOWN

"One of the greatest differences between a failure and a success is that the successful person will tackle chores that the failure avoids".

Og Mandino

wrote "The Greatest Salesman in the World"

Average and below average sales reps love to see the top reps fail. They would rather pull them down off the ladder of success than help push them up. Thus, you must associate with other successful reps rather than "wallow in the mire" with the losers. Those who are failing are always quick to blame everyone but himself or herself. You'll often hear things like: "My territory is too large." "My territory is too small." "The company doesn't understand the customers." "My manager doesn't have a clue." "Our prices are too high." "Our products are antiquated."

When you hear someone whining like this, ask yourself why are other sales people in the company doing just fine? Poor performing sale reps never look inward for the source of their problems, but always look outward for excuses. Always look at what both the successful and unsuccessful sales reps are doing. Emulate the former and avoid the latter.

How many times have you attended a national sales meetings and seen the poorest-performing reps hanging around together complaining about the company, the products and everything else? After my first year in medical sales the two other, driven sales reps within our division left the company. That left me in a division with six or seven average reps. All I wanted to do was work my butt off, keep my manager happy, do my administrative work, win awards, earn commission, and be a good employee.

I'll never forget the reaction of the other reps within my division. They all thought I was a "kiss-up" because I did very well, my manager liked me and I did what was asked of me. Of course, they assumed that I was given special treatment but the reality is that if you are dependent upon your manager for helping you get certain things accomplished; why wouldn't you cooperate with him/her? Why wouldn't you be a good employee? The point is not to worry about what the people at the bottom of the rankings think. Just do the right thing, work hard, and do your best.

There will always be "nay-sayers". There will always be those that want to see you fail. There will always be those who want to pull you off the ladder of success or down to the bottom rungs of failure. I say to you; "fo-get-a-bout it! You, your family, your church or synagogue, your charities, your manager, and the employees inside the organization are depending on you and your success. You just can't worry about what others think. You have to focus on your goals and bottom-line, associate with successful, positive thinking individuals. There are plenty of people out there who want to see you succeed. Focus on them and their positive outlook.

Avoid the losers in your organization but don't be a jerk about it. You should be friendly to everyone. You should be a team player. I believe it is not only the right thing to do but also when you help others it comes back to you ten fold. When those average people reach out in an effort to be better, you should always help them. But, the minute they start to complain or become negative, you need to walk away.

That reminds me of what Abraham Lincoln once said after a friend told him that his enemies were saying terrible things about him. He replied, "I don't care what they say, so long as they're not telling the truth." Be true to yourself and what is right and don't worry what other reps may say.

And it's not only other sales reps who can try to pull you down; customers can too. You may take over a new territory that was "trashed" by a former rep and the first thing the customers want to do is beat you down. It's OK. Let them vent a little. They deserve it that one time. After all, they had to put up with the lousy service of the prior rep and maybe the company took way too long to make a change.

Listen to them vent and then say something similar to the following: "I'm very sorry about your prior experience. It's very unfortunate because I came to XYZ, Inc. because of their fine reputation and the opportunity to represent the best products in the business." If you have been a sales rep in the area for a while, you might add, "I have been in this territory and in this industry for X years and have always provided the highest level of service." In fact, this could be a great opportunity for you to put them in touch with other customers so they can share with them what a great person you are.

Sometimes customers love to bend reality a bit, if doing so will give them an edge. They may say that the former rep gave them product for free when in fact the company consigned the product. He or she may have loaned them the product out of their trunk samples but didn't actually give it to them. I have heard it all. The reality is, that if they were unhappy with the service they were formerly given, they may justify in their minds why they need to bend the truth to get the product for free. But remember, your company, the hospital, and the factory have got to earn money to keep the doors open. Being a good sales rep doesn't mean giving your customers a license to steal – literally or otherwise.

23 | WORK WITH, NOT AGAINST, YOUR MANAGER.

This is an important chapter for both sales reps and sales managers. The sad truth is that only 10-15% of sales reps in the real world do the things necessary to be great sales reps, and the same holds true for managers.

Most companies take their great sales reps and promote them into sales management, with very little training. While I believe that only great sales reps can make great managers, not all great sales reps make great managers. The reason I personally feel only the best reps should become managers is if I'm a great sales rep in the field, why should I listen to the advice or feedback from someone who was only a mediocre sales rep! What are they going to teach me? That's just my opinion. But, I am the first to admit that not all great sale reps make great managers because it takes a certain disposition to be a great manager and not all people have the patience, understanding, or leadership ability to be a great manager.

I can't tell you the amount of times I have spent on the phone with former reps that worked for me, who tell me horror stories about their current managers. I would say that this type of incompetent manager accounts for roughly 10-15% of the managers out there, and yet somehow they seem to keep their jobs way too long. In my opinion, the bell curve for managers is very similar to that for sales reps. Usually, there are 20% great managers, 60% average, and 20% horrible managers.

If you have a horrible manager, there's not much I can tell you. You can either hang in there, and sometimes things will get better, or you might need to find another job. My experience shows that it takes companies about a year to figure out they have a bad manager on their hands. But chances are, most people work for a decent manager, or if you're lucky, a great manager. For those of you with average bosses, my advice is that you learn to work with them. Keep in mind that your success translates into their success. Sometimes they don't realize that, but usually they do. They are not the enemy. Unfortunately, that's how a lot of average sales reps view management, as the enemy.

I have been a manager at four different J&J companies and two other companies as well. In each case, my compensation was based directly on the performance of my sales reps, roughly 50%. So, why would it be in my interest to work against them? Anyone with any common sense, whose income is dependent on the performance of his or her reps, should realize that fact before going into management. In fact, my greatest successes as a manager came when I totally focused on the success of my reps. When I really went to bat for their ideas (those that made sense) is when my management career really took off. I received more awards and recognition than ever before.

Certainly, I never asked for something or did something that wasn't in the best interest of the company. But I began listening more to what those in the trenches were saying rather than be intimidated that "upper management" wouldn't like to hear it or would be upset.

The point is that if you help your manager look good, he or she will work to make you look good. It's human nature. Don't whine and complain. Don't miss their conference calls because, "Things came up" and if you have to miss one, let them know in advance. Don't back door them or go around them to get what you want. Talk to them; don't avoid them. Develop an understanding and working relationship and I guarantee you, just like with customers, it will pay huge dividends. If you need something, present it in a professional manner. Show them the business advantages and reasons for your proposal. Remember: *Your manager is not your enemy but your ally!*

I have found that the reps who avoid their managers, or who hate having them ride in the field with them, are usually hiding something. I always had a blast working with my managers and I usually found that they were there to help me, not to hurt me. They wanted to see me do well because if I did well, they did well. I always try to stress that to my sales reps. Managers don't have all the answers but they are an objective observer who can watch from the outside in and give you feedback that could help you increase sales.

There were nine sales reps in my division with my first medical sales job. All I wanted to do was work hard, sell products, and move up the company ladder. One of my close friends and one of the best sales reps in the company, Doug Elkin, had a similar philosophy. We just kept our noses to the grindstone, and supported our manager. We avoided the inevitable gossip and corporate politics. Of course, most of the other reps, in our division, loved to gossip, and were just average. Because we worked hard and always strived to do well, and to do the right thing, I believe our managers went the extra mile for us.

Of course the other reps viewed us as "kiss-ups" but it didn't matter what they thought. What mattered was whether we were being true to the customers, the company, and ourselves. I tried never to care about what other sales reps thought of me, especially those that didn't perform to the highest level of their ability. You shouldn't worry about them either. Just do your job, do the best you can, and the rest will take care of itself.

One of the greatest sales reps that ever worked for me, Theresa Wood, used to call me to ask about the comp plan, brain storm about opportunities, and talk about her business. I felt she was obsessed with success and I always enjoyed brainstorming with her, as she figured out her way to the top every year. Believe me, she was a success before she met me, I just merely acted as a sounding board. She was always ranked in the top 10%, had won the coveted Sales Rep of the Year Award, many product awards, and many other performance awards as well.

She never whined or complained but was always looking for ways to move the business forward. The point is that Theresa always had a written plan and always knew exactly what she needed to do to get to where she wanted to go. Some managers don't realize how lucky they have it when they have sales reps like Theresa. I always told people that I would "kill" to have ten Theresa's on my team. I'd win Division of the Year every year.

I've worked with top sales reps who were a pain in the neck to work with. I've also hired reps who were fun to be around but I left the company or was promoted prior to their rise to the top. Those listed in my list of "The Best" were there because I enjoyed working with them and they reached the top during our time together. Don't be difficult, as in the long run it will hurt your career. You won't earn as much as you could and you won't gain the recognition because your attitude will sour everyone in the company that might have a say.

24 | GET OTHERS TO RALLY BEHIND YOU

"Great things are not done by impulse, but by a series of small things brought together."

VINCENT VAN GOGH

Some people just don't get it. They are so insecure with their own abilities that they are afraid to be seen or heard by others within the company. Top sales people use all the resources they have at their disposal. They not only call their managers and other reps for help and advice but they call others within the organization to help them to close business as well. They not only bring "things" together to sell product but they also have an ability to bring people together to rally behind them and their cause.

One of the greatest compliments I ever received was from one of my best friends, Dave Perri, who was also one of my two "best men" at my wedding. He said something to the affect that "Dean has an ability to get people to come together and rally behind him or some cause". In fact, all the way back in High School, I was able to rally Dave for his help in my campaign for Senior Class President. He was actually the true mastermind behind my winning the election for Senior Class President in High School.

Now some might say that winning that position was a small accomplishment and it was so long ago, but I truly believe that everything that happens in life happens for a reason and it builds the make-up of who we are. Had I not won that election, thanks to the help of Dave, I might not have become quite as successful in life. Losing could have changed my entire direction. My brilliance was asking Dave to help me. I got him to rally behind me and you need to get others to rally behind you.

Even that experience of losing my job and having to ask a friend to put me up for a short while changed my life. It was the catalyst for me to get my act together and get on with my life and building a career. I think that this is the reason one of my favorite movies of all time was "Back to the Future" with Michael J. Fox. If you have not always had the best experiences in life, and you haven't always had the best luck, you CAN change your course and direction in life. One way to do that is to get others to rally behind you.

In sales, I always make it point to not only be nice to all my customers, but I also try to be nice to my colleagues. A little kindness goes a long way, not only in getting people to rally behind you, but it's also good for your soul. Remember people's birthdays, splurge on lunch for customer service, send thank you notes, give praise publicly, and recognize someone who has given you help in achieving your goals. These are all ways to thank people for being a part of your success. It is also a way to get people to continue helping you.

These little things must all be done with complete and honest sincerity, because if you are only nice to people so that they will help you, they will see right through it. You will be considered a "user"; someone only out for themselves. I had a sales rep that treated people this way and I constantly received negative comments about her from people within the company. On the one hand, she tried to make it appear as though she was so concerned about others; that she was a team player; and that she wanted to help out. That's what she would try to convince others to believe; but her actions would say something else.

Most of my team and others within the organization came to me at one point or another to say that they saw her as being only out for herself. Very few people saw her as one they could trust. She limited her potential because I don't believe people helped her to the highest level they could. If you truly appreciate those with whom you work, they will know it, they will appreciate it, and they will go out of their way to help you.

I don't care how good a sales person you think you are, no one can succeed in sales by themselves. You can get orders for a "ton" of products but if your shipping department doesn't get them out on time, you will fail. If the manufacturing department doesn't make enough products to fill your orders, you will fail. If the marketing department doesn't come up with new products or ways to sell them, you may fail. In short, we are not islands unto ourselves. We are all dependent on each other.

While I am obviously biased towards the importance of good sales people, I do not believe that having a strong sales force, alone, is sufficient for a company to survive and thrive. Sales people, no matter how good, must understand that they need others within the company to support them. Thus, you should treat everyone with respect and try to understand things from their perspective. Work towards supporting them as well.

Write thank you notes and recognize the contributions of others!

One way to get people to rally behind you is to write them a thank you note, either for something specific they did for you or for their work in general. If someone inside your company goes beyond the call of duty, send an email, copying their manager, thanking them for their good work. Getting someone praise from their manager can go a long way to recruiting people on your sales team.

Everyone in life needs a pat on the back, not just sales people. Giving fellow workers recognition might help them get a raise, recognition, or even a promotion someday. For you, the biggest benefit is that they will probably continue going out of their way to help you because they know you appreciate it. If you are unselfish in handing out praise and credit to others, it will come back to you in many ways. I have found that to be true throughout my sales and sales management career.

Sure, it's great to receive recognition yourself. Most sales reps thrive on recognition but so do most everyone else as well; people in all types of jobs. With this in mind, I try to give all the credit for a successful sale to those who helped in the process. If you do this, others will go out of their way to help you. By living this philosophy, you will always be that much more successful and you will receive the biggest recognition of all. You will win the awards, the trips, and all the other things that come with success. And when you walk up on that stage to accept the awards, remember to remember those who helped you along the way.

I once managed a sales rep who was incredibly insecure and paranoid when it came to his sales performance. No matter how much you built him up with recognition, it was never enough. He never helped any of his teammates and he went out of his way to take credit for sales even in other people's territories, whether he helped them or not. In fact, I can't remember a time when he actually helped any one at all.

This guy was a classic; always claiming that he had the toughest territory and that the whole world was out to get him. He just never got it. He was an angry man and his sales always reflected his attitude. He never lived up to his potential and eventually he was let go. To this day, I'm sure he's convinced that the company was wrong and he's still in shock.

Be sure to send thank you notes to your customers as well. Send them thank you notes for buying one of your products, for inviting you to their morning meeting, for their understanding, or for continuing to use the products they bought from you several years ago. Never let too much time go by without letting your customers know just how much they mean to you. After all, it's those customers that buy your products that deserve a tremendous amount of credit for your success.

Rather than try to accomplish everything on your own, figure out what steps you need to take to close the deal, and rally those individuals, within your company, to help you. Stay focused on your task.

Once, I needed an account to be included in a clinical study, in order to get them to begin using my products. It was a real long shot, because they weren't the largest teaching institution, and they didn't have the typical clinical experience for which we normally looked. But I knew it would be good for the company, good for business, and good for the clinical trial, if we got them in the trial, so I was determined to make it happen.

I rallied the Director of Clinical Affairs and the Director of

Business Development, and got them to pay a visit to this account. I threw a dinner party and everyone enjoyed each other's company. We had great presentations and it soon became clear that there was a lot of common ground. They were eventually included in the trial, and we did pick up their business. No one expected us to include the hospital in the trial, but we did, and it was a good thing.

Like all good things, sometimes you can ask for TOO much. You've got to be reasonable and fair to others, or people will not want help you. You can't ask your company to do things that will help you but hurt others within the organization. If you are always unreasonable, always asking for "me, me, me", people will begin to realize your self-centered nature, your reputation will be hurt and people will no longer help you.

At some point, organizations will begin to measure the positive you bring to the company, through your sales dollars, versus the negative you bring by being a troublemaker. If you are a constant complainer, you make it difficult and unfair for others, and you only do things that benefit you, eventually the negative will outweigh the positive. Work to be a team player. Work to help others. Work to recognize others; and others will rally behind you.

Go out of your way to help others to succeed.

Helping others to succeed is not only a good thing to do, but it will help you become a better salesperson. In my experience, training others or sharing ideas requires that you, as the trainer, review the basics as well. Through the cooperation and collaboration with others, you will develop ideas and new sales tactics you may not have thought of alone.

Many people claim they are self-made but don't believe it. Every successful person has had help from others along the way. Get into a positive loop of energy and enthusiasm by helping others succeed. You will receive ten-fold what you give but that shouldn't be the only reason you help others. Help others to help others. It's the right thing to do and in addition, it is incredibly rewarding.

25 READ BOOKS & LISTEN TO AUDIO PROGRAMS TO IMPROVE

"If I had eight hours to chop down a tree, I'd spend six hours sharpening my ax".

ABRAHAM LINCOLN, 16TH PRESIDENT

"Good is the enemy of great".

JIM COLLINS, AUTHOR OF 'FROM GOOD TO GREAT'

You've probably heard it a million times, "the definition of insanity is doing the same things over and over and expecting different results". To be the best, you must continually look for ways to improve and get an edge over your competition. You've got to actively attend and participate in sales training courses, read books, and listen to audio programs to "sharpen your ax".

Each time I took over a new sales team, I would explain to them as a group, that other than the "The Bible", the book that has had the greatest affect on my life was "Think and Grow Rich", by Napoleon Hill. I would always give each of them a copy, and throughout the years, I would constantly reference the book and the power of focusing on written specific goals. It always amazed me that the reps that were always failing or at the bottom of the sales rankings never even opened the first page. The best reps would always call me and tell me how much they got out of it and how much they enjoyed it.

When I was Director of Sales and Marketing at one company, I went to work in the field with the sales rep who was at the very bottom of the rankings. When I asked him if he had read the book, he replied like so many other failing reps before him, "I read the first few chapters but I just haven't had the time to finish it". I just couldn't believe what I was hearing but then again I shouldn't have been surprised. I said to him, "You know, if I was at the bottom of the rankings and someone suggested that a certain book had the biggest impact on his selling career, I would have MADE the time to read it immediately.

Sometimes I wonder what people are thinking. If any top sales rep or manager tells me that a certain sales book or self help book was the 2nd greatest book they ever read on improving their life, I would go out and read it immediately. Why? If someone feels that strongly about a book, there must be some terrific "gems" within its pages. If one word, sentence or paragraph can help me improve, so I can get that much farther ahead in life, then it was worth the time and the cost to read it.

Many call that "sharpening" your ax. It comes from the story of the young lumberjack who early on, in his career, could chop down more trees than anyone within 200 miles. He was bigger and stronger than all the other lumberjacks and his ability to quickly chop down a tree was admired all over the land. But as the weeks went on, the daily number of trees he cut down got smaller and smaller and smaller.

The young man just couldn't figure out what was happening. Instead of his job getting easier and easier, it began to get harder and harder. Each night he was wiped out from exhaustion. Finally, an older lumberjack, who was watching him for months, sat him down and told him, "See here boy, its not always how strong you are or how hard you work. What's important is that you always keep your ax sharp. You've got to take time to sharpen your ax."

As we discussed, hard work is a key ingredient of success. The reality is that if you work hard, but also look for ways to improve your efficiency, you can increase sales without exhausting yourself or worse, burning yourself out. You've got to take time to read sales and self-improvement books, and take time to call other successful reps and find out what they are doing. *Never stop learning.*

The other common trait I find among average or below average sales reps is that they DON'T seem to talk to anyone else within the company. They don't touch base with their manager unless the manager calls them. They don't call their associates. They don't call the product directors for ideas. They don't seem to brainstorm with anyone. They're just happy doing the same things they have always done. When they do call their teammates, it's to complain or whine. They complain about everything: the comp plan, their products, the car allowance, their manager, or their customers.

Ralph Larsen, the former CEO of Johnson and Johnson, said, "The only thing inevitable is change and if we rest on our laurels, and don't change, we will become dinosaurs." Big companies are not the only things that can become dinosaurs – so can sales reps. You must be willing to change, to grow and adapt. To do this, you must keep "your ax sharp".

One of my favorite expressions states, "If you keep doing the same things you've always done, you'll keep getting the same results you've always got." In other words, if you find yourself at the bottom of the sales rankings, start to look inward at yourself for the explanation, rather than blaming others. Start to improve yourself and your sales will improve.

Why is it, that at every national training meeting, it's always the top reps, sitting in the front row, taking copious notes and doing everything they can do to get "one up" on their competition? The weakest reps are always late getting to the meetings and they are late coming back from the breaks. In addition, they never take a single note. This just happened again, at the most recent national sales meeting I attended. My best reps were writing away, and contributing to the discussions, while my weakest rep sat there in a daze.

26 | RULE OF 72; ANOTHER REASON TO BE THE BEST

"The greatest mathematical discovery of all time is compound interest."

ALBERT EINSTEIN

One friend asked, after reading this book, "Why include this chapter in a book on becoming a top sales rep?" Again, I hope most of you in sales have the goal of being a top commission earner. This chapter is just another motivation in achieving this goal. In addition, I believe this concept is so important for anyone in this world to understand, as to give hope to all those feeling they can never retire or live their final years in comfort.

Many people in this great country of opportunity do not understand that anyone can eventually become wealthy at some point in their life. It may take them until retirement or it could happen when they are younger but most people CAN become wealthy. They say that less than 5% of the American population can retire without some sort of financial assistance. I don't feel this is necessary but people don't realize they can make it happen. It's a fact that with written specific goals, and the compounding of money, most people can at least retire comfortably. While it may take a while, don't procrastinate in your journey to prepare for retirement. Take the first step by putting $5, $10, or something away each paycheck.

This chapter will hopefully provide you with another great reason to strive to be the best sales rep you can be, as well as a reason to strive to be the #1 rep within your company. When I was 29, broke, and out of a job, I had never been taught the "Rule of 72". I had made the decision that I would never be broke again, but at the time I did not understand the power of compounding returns and how quickly one could accumulate wealth. In fact, I believe that even those who aren't in sales or who don't make big commission checks can retire wealthy, if they understand this principal and work to put some money away.

I am not an accountant or a financial advisor. I'm not guaranteeing that if you follow these concepts you will become wealthy in any given amount of time. But put them to good use and you will have a much better chance than if you do nothing. Talk to an accountant. Talk to a financial advisor, but whatever you do, don't let anyone steal away your dreams.

What is the Rule of 72 and why do I believe it is the key to financial freedom and wealth?

The Rule of 72 is a mathematical formula for calculating how long it takes to double your money and it's really quite simple. To find out how long it takes to double your money, simply divide the number 72 by your investment's overall rate of return. Keep in mind that the Rule of 72 is a mathematical fact and not "smoke and mirrors". If you work it out on a piece of paper, you will see that it is true. In fact, I have provided some examples for you in this chapter to prove it to you.

For instance, if you are getting a 10% return on your investments, it will take you 7.2 years to double your money. If you are getting a 15% return, it will take you 4.8 years to double your money. If you are getting a 20% return, it will take you 3.6 years to double your money, etc. etc. It's incredible. I only wish I knew about it when I was 12, 16, or even 18. I would have done things a lot differently but the point is that it is never too late to start. If you never get started, you may die broke and penniless. If you are 50 today, with today's medical therapies, you may very well live to be over 100, so don't feel it is worthless to begin the process now.

As a sales rep, assume you'll earn $100,000 a year for the next 10 years. You might think that your tax rate will be 30-32%, but few realize that all of your income is not taxed at that rate. Your "net effective rate" (average rate) may be closer to 20%. The reason is that not all of your income is taxed at 32%. The first $10,000 is taxed at a much lower rate, the next $10,000 at another slightly higher rate, all the way up to the last portion being taxed at the 32%. Then, after you deduct all your business expenses and other deductibles your net effective rate may be closer to 20%-25%. It is only the highest level of your income that is taxed at 30-32%, while the lower levels are taxed at lower tax rates; plus the deductions. Make sure you understand this and if you don't, talk to an accountant before you move on.

Let's assume your average or net effective tax rate is 20%. Let's use that amount for this example. With an income of $100,000 your "after tax" income will be $80,000. ($100,000 times 20% equals $20,000 in taxes). Now, commit yourself to living off $50,000 of that remaining $80,000. I realize it may be impossible to live off $50,000, especially if you are married. However, in Florida, where I began my career at age 29, I lived off less than that. Thus, if you live off $50,000, you'll save $30,000 a year.

If you save $30,000 for 5 years, you will have saved $150,000 before you calculate any return. (5 ⋆ $30,000 = $150,000) but you'll actually have much more than that because your money will be compounding and growing during those five years. Let me take you through the whole thing so you truly understand and believe in the rule of 72.

Year 1 $30,000

Year 2 $30,000 x 10% = $3,000 + 30,000 + 30,000 = $63,000

Year 3 $63,000 x 10% = $6,300 + $63,000 + 30,000 = $99,300

Year 4 $99,300 x 10% = $9,930 + 99,300 + 30,000 = $139,230

Year 5 $139,230 x 10% = $13,923 + 139,230 + $30,000 = **$183,153**

So, now you understand that instead of having $150,000 after 5 years, by saving $30,000 per year, you'll actually have almost $185,000. Not to be confusing, but you will actually have even more than

$185,000, because you'll be saving the money monthly, when you get your monthly commission checks. Hence the money will compound monthly, not annually, giving you even more at the end of five years.

Now, let me prove to you that the rule of 72 really works. Assume you said to yourself, "I'm going to bust my butt for 5 years, save $200,000 and then I'm never saving another dime. Let me show you how, by the time you retire, you can have quite a lot of money. To make it simple, I'll start with $200,000 at a 10% rate of return. So, in 7.2 more years, based on the rule of 72, I need to prove to you that you'll double your money. This will be in the 13th year from the point of this discussion. It took you 5 years to save the money and 7.2 more years to double it.

And so it goes:

Year 6 $200,000 x 10% = $20,000 + $200,000 = $220,000

Year 7 $220,000 x 10% = $22,000 + $220,000 = $242,000

Year 8 $242,000 x 10% = $24,200 + $242,000 = $266,200

Year 9 $266,200 x 10% = $26,620 + $266,200 = $292,820

Year 10 $292,820 x 10% = $29,282 + $292,820 = $322,102

Year 11 $322,102 x 10% = $32,210 + $322,102 = $354,312

At the end of year 12, you'll have:

Year 12 $354,312 x 10% = $35,431 + $354,312 = $389,743

In 2/10 of one more year, you will have doubled your $200,000. Remember, it wasn't 7 years to double your money. It was 7.2 years. So, in about the middle of March, 7.2 years after you obtained the $200,000 you will have doubled your money.

At the end of the 13th year, you'll have:

$389,743 x 10% = $38,974 + $389,743 = $428,717. So, now do you believe me? The Rule of 72 is a mathematical fact.

Now, this is where the fun begins. If you have $400,000 in 13.2 years; you'll double it again in another 7.2 years for a total of $800,000. This will take you a total of 20.4 years. In another 7.2 years, you'll have $1,600,000. That will be in 27.6 years. Finally, in another 7.2 years, you'll have $3,200,000. That will be in 34.8 years. Let's assume you began this project when you were 25 years old. By the time you are 60 years old, you'll have almost $2.5 million dollars and **that's assuming you quit saving after you obtained the $200,000 after the first five years.**

I can keep going if you like. When you are 67 and retired, you'll have a cool $5 mil. If you continue saving after the first five years, you'll have a lot more than $5 million when you hit 67. In addition, over the last 15 years, even after the dot.gone crash, I've been able to get a return of closer to 15% on my total portfolio, including other investments besides stocks.

Go back and re-figure the numbers at 15%, doubling your money every 5 years.

Year 10	$400,000
Year 15	$800,000
Year 20	$1,600,000
Year 25	$3,200,000

Now, you've hit $3,200,000 by the time you are 50, instead of $2,500,000 when you are 60. When you are 55, you'll have a cool $6.4 mil. When you are 60, you'll have $13 mil, and finally when you are 65, you'll have $26mil. I don't want to make it seem unrealistic, but the bottom line is that the sky is the limit. Start now, earning and saving.

These are only a few examples of the power of compounded interest. I had many more examples, originally in the book, but a few people commented, "Dean, enough already with the Rule of 72". You know how much you earn each year and how much you can save. Use your own figures. Allow yourself to dream. Play with the formula. My examples were conservative. Push the limit. Go for it. Some day you can sell coconuts, live off that coconut money and watch your savings continue to explode. I'm not saying you can necessarily retire at 50, but keep working hard, keep saving, without touching your principal, and you will be on the path to financial freedom at some point in your life.

One of the biggest points to take away from this exercise is that the more you save today, the faster your money will grow. The longer you wait to start saving, the longer it will take you to become a millionaire, financially free, or achieve any of your financial goals. But isn't it amazing that with just a little goal setting it is possible to become a millionaire in just 10, 15 or 20 years? Most people figure they can never become wealthy so they never try.

Now I know it's not that easy. You want to live your life and enjoy it today. Believe me, after 9/11, there's a lot to be said for that. It's not easy to save. You have families, with college tuition, etc. You need a vacation. It comes down to however much you want to sacrifice and save, determines how much you have at the end. I realize and you should also remember that you don't take any of it with you when you die, so you must live. Thus, my wife and I are enjoying ourselves but we also save. I personally, don't want to be relying on the government or my children to be taking care of me when I get old.

Another important fact in reaching your financial goals is to be sure to maximize your 401k if your company offers one. Some companies match their employee's savings into the 401k at 50 cents to the dollar. For every dollar you put into the 401k, they put in 50 cents on your behalf. Think about it. That's a 50% return right off the bat. Even better yet, some companies match 75 cents, which is an immediate 75% return. Some companies even match 100% dollar for dollar giving you a 100% return. I do not believe you should decide which company for which to work based on whether they have a good 401k or not, as there are many more important factors to consider. But if they have one, take advantage of it.

Now in the case of Johnson and Johnson, the stock itself has earned roughly 18 -20% over the last 20 years or so. Add that onto their 75% match, and I was getting roughly a 95% return on the money invested in the 401k. 72 divided by 95 is .75, thus about every year, you are doubling your money. So, if you earn $150,000 and can invest 6% in a 401k, that's $9,000. You'd be doubling your money, about every 9 months. You can see how fast your retirement savings can build up in a 401k, because remember, it's tax-deferred.

Now, not everyone will become a millionaire in 20 years, based on this formula, because everyone's situation in life may differ. People may earn less than $100,000 and/or it may be impossible to live off $30,000-$50,000 per year. There may be a few soft years in which your rate of return may be less than 10%, but I believe that everyone can, in a lifetime, retire a millionaire. It will require hard work, written goals, and planning but you can do it. Obviously, the more you make, and the greater your rate of return, the faster it will happen.

Understand that you must set your goal to earn as much money as you can TODAY. Dedicate yourself to maximizing your income over the next five to ten years and you are well on your way to wealth.

Settle for average or below average and you may never be able to retire. But strive to achieve wealth and financial security, and you will be able to provide your family with the best that life has to offer.

27 | STAY FOCUSED ON ONE THING

"Consider the postage stamp. It secures success through its ability to stick to one thing until it gets there."

JOSH BILLINGS

One mistake many people make is they get so focused on becoming millionaires, as fast as possible, that they get themselves involved in too many things at once. This is very dangerous and at the end of ten years, you may not have accumulated any wealth nor will you be a great sales rep. The key is to focus on one thing and get really good at it. If you want to be a great real estate investor, focus on that. If you want to be a top sales rep, focus on that.

I've seen people who were in sales, who day-traded during their sales time, did real estate on the side, and all sorts of other things. They wound up being average with all of them and below average as a sales rep. In order to be the best at what you do, you must focus on one thing. Pursuing any type of outside business dealings, during your career job will ultimately lead to failure and possibly to losing your job.

28 DRESS FOR SUCCESS; DON'T DO THINGS THAT MAY ALIENATE CUSTOMERS

No one likes to buy from a slob. If you dress like you are successful, people will believe you are successful. When a car dealer wants to sell a used car what does he do? He repaints the car, details the interior, steam cleans the engine, and gets it out on the lot. Well, you are a product of the company in a sense. You need to make sure you are presentable. Don't wear trendy, over-the-top clothes. Don't paint your hair a weird color or grow a goatee. Whatever you want to do on your free time is your business, but if your appearance could offend even one customer, it's not worth it. You are in sales to sell a lot of product and make a lot of money. If making a political, societal, or fashion statements is so important to you, get into arts and entertainment or some other line of work.

I had a rep working in my sales force who was a terrific guy. He was very bright, had tremendous clinical knowledge and people really liked him. But he had this bleached, almost white hair. He wore funky bowling shoes, and "Hollywood Glasses". You know the kind. The thin black frames, often with colored lenses. As great a guy as he was, I just know there were older, conservative surgeons who thought he looked ridiculous. Now if he lost credibility with 10% of his customers how much did his fashion statements cost him and the company?

Even if you end up Sales Rep of the Year, if you could have increased your sales by another 10% by just conforming a little, is it worth making some crazy fashion statement? I don't think so. In all my years in medical sales, I can't remember a Sales Rep of the Year that looked wild and crazy. Later, this guy went on to another division, and the next time I saw him, he had gone back to his normal hair color and had a much more conservative look. Somehow, either he figured it out or someone told him.

On the weekends I sometimes look like an entirely different person. First, I tend to dress "way" down in a sort of "beach bum" motif. In addition, I can grow a goatee in about 2 days. But when I'm in front of the customer, I keep it conservative. I suggest you keep it conservative as well. Wear button-down shirts, business suits, no facial hair, and have a short, normal haircut. If you don't care about image, play the game for ten years, become financially independent, and grow a ponytail for all I care. I'm all about maximizing my chances of selling more. If you want to be a top sales rep, you should too.

I also realize that wearing suits may not apply to your industry. If you are selling construction products, calling on job sites, you might get chased off the property if you show up in a suit. Boots may be in order. Just be sure you wear the appropriate attire for your industry. If all your top associates wear boots, don't show up in leather sandals. If everyone in your industry wears sport coats, don't show up in a golf shirt. Most sales jobs require suits, so don't try to be a trend setter. Enough said!

29 | TRY TO BE DIFFERENT THAN ALL THE OTHERS

When choosing how to dress at work, don't be different. In all other ways, try to be different. During interviews, I often ask prospective employees to, "tell me about the most unique thing you have done to be different from other reps". What have you truly done to set yourself apart from the competition?" Usually, I get horrible answers, including things that people should do in the course of their jobs anyway. One woman told me that she goes out of her way to educate the nurses about her products. Every top medical sales rep should be doing this. That's like a copier rep saying they "educate the people in the offices about how to run a copier machine". These things just aren't impressive.

Doing something unique is spending your weekend, in the account, learning from your key customer. One rep told me she volunteered and actually baby-sat her customer's kids. Now I'm not suggesting that anyone go that far, but obviously this rep was willing to go the extra mile to build relationships with her customers.

A customer paged one rep on the weekend because the copier he sold them broke down. They had an important job that they were working on, so he left his family outing to deliver a loaner unit. He also spent a few hours helping them make copies, so they could catch up and not waste their entire weekend.

There are many ways you can go above and beyond the call of duty. When you do, your customers will never forget it. Dare to be different. Don't just bring in donuts, like everyone else; be creative. Remember, you don't have to do it on your own or come up with the ideas. Find out what other successful people are doing and then put your own twist on it.

I've seen reps make pancakes for the customers. Sounds a little cheesy but the customers loved it and talked about it for weeks. I've learned a lot from so many great reps with whom I've worked. Great reps don't always try to pave the way themselves. As we discussed in other chapters, learn from the best. Use the techniques that other successful reps are using. Stay in touch with the top reps. Always work to be different. Many advanced sales jobs don't require you to do these things. But I have still seen my advanced reps do little things to separate themselves as well.

One sales rep I knew would bring in "coffee charge cards" to his customer's office staff. This made them extremely happy and helped them to overlook his many phone calls to find out the surgery schedules. He became Rookie of the Year that first year. Another rep would bring in candy into the OR and leave it in a jar with the company logo on it. If any other sales rep dared to put candy in her jar, they would be ostracized for a long time.

These examples surround building relationships, but you should also be creative and unique in your sales presentations. Find some new or exciting way to demonstrate your products. Brighten someone's day. Figure out a fun way to get them involved with the presentation. SEPARATE YOURSELF from the rest!

30 | UNDERSTAND THE PSYCHOLOGY OF SELLING

This topic is a little harder to teach and a little harder to understand. I do not believe you should ever "trick" your customers or lie to your customers to get them to buy your products. But, if your product meets their needs and they are being unreasonable, there is nothing wrong with using a little reverse psychology to win them over. This is not trickery but rather understanding human nature and using it to your advantage. It takes confidence and timing to pull this off, thus you've got to make sure you are ready to walk away from a sale. You will know when it is the right time to use various statements or techniques such as this.

One such time is when you sense someone is just merely trying to "beat you up" and would rather see a win-lose situation rather than a win-win situation. For example, many times I've had to deal with a difficult customer who just seems to hem and haw. You know the type, someone who seems to question every little thing and just can't make a decision. Often they just enjoy seeing you bend over backwards until you break. As I gained confidence in my career and ability, I would get to a point in which I would just turn, look them in the eye and say, "Maybe this product just isn't right for you" or "Maybe this just isn't the right time for you to get involved with this technology" and I meant it.

This technique is especially effective when you know you have a fantastic product that deep down you know they want. If you appear as though you are ready to walk, customers will often turn their attitudes right around. People want what they can't have. It's just a fact of human nature.

I used this technique many times while selling capital equipment for one company. This is not a trick or a misleading technique. I would get to the end of my rope and rather than be rude, I'd just throw that out there. I sold three units over the phone this way!

Another example came early in my career. There was a customer in Southwest Florida that wasn't buying any of my products. I had been trying to get my foot in the door for months. In 1990, Laparoscopic surgery was just taking off which requires many cords and instruments to lie on the surgical field. My company came out with a very clever surgical drape that had Velcro straps all around it, to keep expensive instrument from falling on the floor. It was about double the cost of a regular drape. We were selling them so fast that we couldn't keep them in stock, so we needed them to buy a case to try rather then us just giving them one free.

I finally got this customer to order in the product. Rather than give in to their demands of a free sample, I offered them a money back guarantee if for some reason they didn't like the product. They loved the product and it became a permanent addition to their supplies. It's the little things sometimes that can make the difference.

Two points to take away: First, never, if possible, give away free product. Psychologically, people "buy" into your product more if they buy evaluation product. Any time I did give away free product, it usually sat on someone's desk for weeks, unless I followed up to ensure they used the product. Don't waste your time or your company's money. I realize sometimes there is no way to avoid it but you must fight the urge to just give it away. That's the easy way out and it usually fails.

Second, always be there when your product is being used for the first time. Again, psychologically, you have a better chance in making the conversion or the sale by being there to hold the customer's hand. Inevitably, if you aren't there, they will use it wrong and they will then be unhappy with your product. It never fails. The customer will always say, "There's no need for you to be here. We've used similar products before. Why in the world would we need you to be here for this?" But don't fall for it. Inevitably, things will go wrong if you're not there.

Gaining your customer's confidence is probably the strongest psychological tool you can employ. And sometimes that requires doing things that might not seem to make much sense. For example, you might recommend a competitor's product, when it is truly superior to yours. You must be very careful when you use this technique and it certainly depends on what type of product you are selling. If you are selling copiers, certainly you don't want to recommend your competitor's. If you are selling Fords, you don't want to recommend a Chevy to your customers. I'm talking about inexpensive products that can benefit patients or customers.

I have used this technique several times, which helped me convert every stick of business but that one minor product. People respect others who are honest and those who truly care about the well being of them and/or their patients.

There is an art to how you position things with people. I believe it can be learned but many people struggle with their ability to "read the customer" and with their ability to "physiologically" sell. There is a "soft" approach, which can relax the customer, gain their trust; and it gets them to open up. There are questions you can ask that expand your customers thinking. Again, this is harder to teach, but watch other successful reps that are "smooth" when they speak. Listen to the way they pepper their discussions with little statements that build trust with the customer. Trust is everything in sales.

One final discussion in the realm of "psychology" should be so basic, but I must mention it anyway: "THE CUSTOMER IS ALWAYS RIGHT". Pretty "deep" psychology, eh?

Always remember who the customer is. To me, it's amazing how many people treat customers poorly. Don't get angry with customers. Don't argue with them. Don't talk back or down to them. *They are the customers; you are the salesman.* You don't have to let them treat you disrespectfully; but always remember who they are. If a customer is rude or disrespectful, you can merely say, "I've obviously caught you at a bad time so I will try you later." If someone is really being abusive, you can quietly and calmly let them know that you are leaving and will try them back at a better time. Usually, they will calm down and you may find they later apologize.

If they refuse to calm down, you've just got to walk away from it because in the end, no matter what you do, YOU LOSE. Be the bigger person and keep your cool. You may gain a loyal customer. If you don't like losing arguments, join a debate club. But remember, you are in sales and arguing with customers is a losing proposition. You will never win trying to defend yourself, the customer service department, your quality control department, or whatever it might be that angered your customer. If you or your company is wrong, admit it immediately and work fast to correct the situation. Just handle the situation calmly and let them know you appreciate their feedback. Usually, angry customers merely want to know that someone is listening to them and they will take action.

Have you ever called a company to complain about something and the person on the other line is polite and understanding. They make statements like, "I understand how you feel", "I would be upset as well". They let you know they are taking down the information and will either do something about it or report it to the higher authorities. It is almost impossible to get angry with them. On the other hand, if you get someone with an attitude that tries to defend the company or the situation, it makes you angrier and angrier. After the conversation, if you have another choice of product or service, you usually don't go back. Well, the same thing holds true for face-to-face selling.

If your customer is wrong, just bite your lip. People don't like to be proven wrong, especially if they are the customers. In many types of sales jobs, you only have so many customers, so you can't go around alienating half of them. If you don't think you can handle it, get a desk job. Part of being a great sales rep is having the ability to see the perspective of the customer; to allow them to vent; and to be a good listener. No matter what company you work for, I can guarantee you, there will be back orders, price increases, recalls, or other irritants to you customers. Accept it and deal with it. Remember, many times in sales, you are making double what the person yelling at you is earning, so just take stock in that fact and let them vent. In the end, when they buy your products, you win.

The chance you will change someone's mind, when they are angry or frustrated, is slim. Arguing will probably just cause them to dig their heals in deeper and they will either quit giving you new business or they might even switch your existing business just to prove whose boss.

31 | BE ACCOUNTABLE AND TAKE RESPONSIBILITY FOR YOUR SUCCESS OR FAILURES. NO EXCUSES.

I am the master of my fate; the captain of my soul.
WILLIAM ERNEST HENLEY

Observe successful people and you'll see they have many common traits, like a positive attitude and a burning desire to succeed. Observe failures and they have common traits as well. The biggest one that comes to mind is their need to make excuses rather than trying to figure out what they might be doing wrong. Successful people rarely make excuses. If your sales numbers aren't good, don't make excuses or blame others. Look inward. Figure out what you might be doing wrong. Be open to coaching, advice and feedback from your manager.

My feeling is that every territory in the world has its unique challenges. The great reps find ways to get around or through those challenges. They look under every rock and don't stop until they have flushed out every opportunity and sales possibility. You have become great when you realize that no one is to blame for your success or failure but YOU. Sure, when you succeed, there are many people to thank, who contributed, but ultimately YOU made it happen. Everything you achieve or become or didn't achieve and didn't become is up to YOU.

I saw a funny t-shirt the other day that read, "Life isn't short: it's just that death is forever". Instead of retiring wealthy and feeling as though you have succeeded in your career, you may retire unsatisfied and maybe without enough to make ends meet. You will be angry at the world and you will blame the world instead of yourself. So when you are struggling, rather than blame everyone else, look in the mirror and ask yourself what you can do to change so that you can reach your full potential. Use the chapters of this book as a checklist and begin doing the things that will make you a top, successful sales rep.

"If you want the rainbow, you've gotta put up with the rain."
Dolly Parton, great singer and an all-around nice person

Dolly Parton would have been an incredible sales person. She is genuine, upbeat, positive, driven, and she has a great personality. You can tell she really cares about people and she would have cared about her customers; had she been in sales.

In their study of the most common characteristics of top sales-people, the Harvard Business School found that the top sales reps take total responsibility for their results. They don't blame the company, their manager, their territory, their father, their mother or the government. They make themselves accountable; whether things are good or bad.

Having been a sales rep in Florida and California, and having sold or watched people sell in almost every other state in the U.S., I can tell you that every territory, state, and region has it's unique challenges. Having also managed reps across the country, I have heard every excuse in the book, from average or below average reps. The "winners", those top reps that get on stage year after year, somehow manage to find opportunity no matter what challenges they face.

Life isn't always easy. In fact, many times it's down right tough. But you are not alone out there. When the tough times come, use all the resources around you. You've got to remember that everyone is facing challenges and roadblocks. You've just got to keep your nose to the grindstone, stay positive and keep moving forward. Success takes hard work and sacrifice.

At some point, you have to take accountability and responsibility.

You have to reflect and say, what am I doing wrong. What am I doing or not doing that other successful reps have mastered in this business? I hate being in the position of laying the cards on the table. It is the worst part of being a manager but it is a necessary part of the job. I always feel horrible in these situations but I have to stop and ask myself, "Whose fault is it?" It is all very frustrating and disappointing.

If you are performing way below the national average, at some point you must quit lying to yourself and quit coming up with excuses as to why you are failing. It's like déjà vu, every time I work with a struggling rep. The faces have been changed to protect the guilty. It's the same thing every time. Any suggestions you have, they've already done them. They are always defensive and they resist change.

Always be accountable for your performance.

32 | YOU'VE GOT TO SELL NEW PRODUCTS

"The journey of a thousand miles begins with a single step."

ANCIENT PROVERB

New products are the life-blood of any company. Anyone can sell the tried and true products. There's no creativity to doing what's been done before. But companies need you to get out there and sell the new products that help drive profitability. Not only is it a benefit to the company and customer but it is also a benefit to you. Selling new products gives you something to talk about and it allows you to differentiate yourself from the competition. You are bringing value to your customers.

Some people are afraid to fail with new products but all it often takes is that first step of pulling them out of "the bag".

No excuses! Sell new products.

People who can't sell new products always have a million excuses. The rest of the country is selling the "pants" off of them, but somehow, the reps with zero sold always have unique conditions in their territories, that won't allow them to sell the new products. I've heard them all. "My doctors trained with Dr. "so and so" and they use the product he designed. They will never switch"; "No one in my territory is using that approach"; "There are no older patients in my territory, so *I can't sell the product*"; "Managed care has taken over here, worse than anywhere else, so *I can't sell the product*"; "The moon isn't quite aligned with Venus yet, so *I can't sell the product*". See a pattern here?

Look around the rest of the country. If no one is selling the product, then maybe there is a problem with it, but if everyone else is selling it, you better get a move on it. My experience in selling and managing is that every territory has unique and sometimes similar issues and challenges. Find a way to make it happen. Look under every rock. Turn every stone. If no one is doing that procedure or technique, then get people trained. Bring in speakers. Send people to courses. No matter what industry you work in, think creatively, think out of the box, brainstorm with your manager and other successful reps and figure out a way to make it happen. No excuses. The top sales reps find a way to get it done. Losers make excuses.

33 | DON'T JUST LET COMPETITORS TAKE BUSINESS; PUT UP A FIGHT

"In the middle of difficulty lies opportunity".
ALBERT EINSTEIN (1879-1955)

Meeting a competitive challenge immediately and aggressively is the best way to protect your territory, and may be the only way to get business back once you've lost it. You may have to go see a few end users, resell them on your product, and get them to ask for your product back. But, if you are there right away and they see your face, they may realize or remember what a great rep you are. You can remind them why they used your product in the first place, and you'll have a much better chance of getting them to back your product and you.

You must fight the battles to win the war! If you think a competitive threat is just going to go away, you're terribly mistaken. As painful as threats are, you must defend your business. Great reps always do.

Hopefully, you will know about competitive threats before they happen. The best way to do that is by visiting customers on a regular basis. Reading reports is one way to spot a trend but it won't always tell you the full story. Remember, if you catch it on a report, you may already be 30 or 60 days late. Actually being in the account, talking to "live" human beings is always the best defense but reviewing reports provides a backup. If they sneak the competitive product in without you knowing about it, you can also catch it by watching the trends on your sales report. I can't tell you how many times it allowed me to see negative trends and nip competitive threats in the bud. If you don't catch downward trends in time, the customers will settle in with other products.

If you have lost business and you have fought as hard as you possibly can to save the business; you learned and presented the necessary clinical or technical papers to defend your business; and there is nothing more you can do, then moving on to new opportunities is justified. Sometimes, even after you've lost business and you feel you've done everything, two months later a problem can occur with the competitive product. If you have kept in touch with the account, you might have an opportunity to still get the business back. Right the account off for two years, and you may never get back in.

The mistake some reps make in every industry and every company is to NOT FIGHT when they have a competitive threat. That is part of being a great sales rep and it's a part of the job. You may not have a competitive threat for a year after launching a new product in your territory, but sooner or later you will. When it happens, you must be prepared to defend the business. While it is uncomfortable, you must fight.

I knew a rep in Florida, who had competitive threats in every single account in her territory. The threats weren't just local; they were a national problem. The other company was selling on price. Due to "managed care" in the early 90's, material managers were forcing physicians to try cheaper products.

Many reps might have thrown in the towel. When all your customers care about is price, and yours isn't the least expensive product, you could have a problem; but not this rep. One by one, she got into the accounts, talked to the customers and presented them with information, not just once, but over and over and over. She planted the seeds of doubt, even though it was very uncomfortable. Every material manager yelled at her, but it was her job and her responsibility to the patients to ensure the doctors knew the facts. One by one, she defeated every single competitive threat.

Why did she have this drive to fight? One reason, she was driven by the desire to be the #1 rep in the country. Another reason was because she passionately believed in her products and knew they were better for her customers. Hospitals were bringing in the competitive product merely for cost savings and it was bad for the patients. The customers had not received a lot of this information, thus it was her job to make sure it was in their hands. If she did not get the information and data into their hands, then she would have failed. The competitive product would have remained in the accounts longer, until it became painfully obvious to her customers that they had made a costly mistake.

It is our responsibility to ensure the customers have the true facts, information and data as well. This allows them to make informed decisions. The bottom line is we must not trade business. We shouldn't work so hard to gain business in one account, and then let it slip away in another account. This is trading business, which is not only expensive and time-consuming, it is counter-productive.

Eventually, if you don't combat the threats in each account, the competition will work their way around to the newly gained accounts. As you continue to lose business, eventually there won't be anywhere else to go to pick up new business. Yes, it will be uncomfortable sometimes, and people won't appear receptive. However, you must always keep fighting, keep believing, and you will win.

34 | IF YOU NEED HELP, ASK FOR IT

Recently, I had to do the hardest thing that a sales manager must do. Having just started a new management job, my company at the time, decided that one of my reps was not doing the job, had not asked for help, was incompetent, and needed to go. They asked me to put him on a performance plan.

The problem was that I was new to the company and didn't really know this person. So, the first thing I did was to get out and work with him and assess his abilities myself. I did not go out with the intent of putting him on a performance plan but rather to gauge his strengths and weaknesses for myself, rather than rely on what others said. I have always believed that you should listen to what other people say, take their input but, in the end, you must form your own opinion. This is particularly true if you are the manager and are responsible for evaluating people. I form my own opinion and decision before doing something that will affect the lives of not only the people that work for me but for their families as well.

If, after giving them the benefit of the doubt, they still fail to get motivated and to do the things they need to do to be successful, then as a manager, we must unfortunately do the tough things that are best for the customers, the company, and really, for the sales rep as well.

Unfortunately, it became very obvious, after several field visits that this guy wasn't working and was taking advantage of the company. I soon put him on a performance plan but I didn't necessarily do it to fire him. In fact, the times that I have put people on plans, I truly did it with the intent of helping them save their job.

After reviewing his weekly reports, I observed three things. First, in the past year, this rep had not asked for any help. Even though the weekly sales reports had a section called "Help Needed" this guy had never put one comment down in that section. Second, the rep had lost over 50% of his business in that preceding year! Third, none of the customers in the territory knew who he was except for two or three. That's a problem.

For heaven's sake, if you find yourself lost or unable to make the right moves, ask for help. Top sales people don't allow this to happen. They are so obsessed with success that within a few weeks of being out in their territory, if they determine they need help, they ask for it.

IF YOU NEED HELP, ASK FOR IT!

35 | GET OUT AND SEE THE CUSTOMERS

"Over the years I've watched individual salespeople who somehow find ways to rise above their peers. They have many traits that are consistent with success, but one habit that stands out far above anything else is the fact that they're constantly making calls on customers."

CHARLES LAUER, PUBLISHER, MODERN HEALTHCARE

80% of success is showing up.

WOODY ALLEN

While this chapter may be somewhat repetitive, it is so important, it deserves review. So many people fail in sales because they just don't get out and see the customers. They procrastinate, which is one of the worst traits that leads to failure. They sit in their office and spend hours getting organized. Being organized is a good thing but don't over do it. If many procastinators would just spend all that time they wasted going out and seeing their customers, they would double or triple their sales.

Many times people waste time and procrastinate because of their fear of failure and rejection. I hate to use an overused but true cliché but sales is a numbers game. The more you get out and see customers, and show them product, the more business you are going to close. Of course, in addition to going to see the customers, as we mentioned in other chapters, you've got to have an objective for each call. You have got to "pull your products out of the bag" and get them into the hands of the end-user. Shaking hands and bringing in donuts just isn't going to "cut it". You've got to SELL your products.

One failing sales rep, working on a new sales team I managed, realized the "jig" was up. I sensed he wasn't working and he knew I sensed it. After he had left the company, a candidate for the position informed me that he happened to have been in a major account with this former rep and no one knew him. I could tell, the first time I worked with him, he wasn't working. He just wasn't getting out there and meeting the customers. He could have had an incredible career but he just wasn't going to work every day, nor was he going out to see his customers.

For the few months he remained, and began calling on customers, his sales took off. He just didn't have the passion to keep it going long term.

While I have given you some pretty good tips that I have picked up over the years, most of this book, and any sales book, is just common sense. It isn't rocket science but yet so many fail to do the things necessary to succeed. Again, "the top sales reps merely do the things others don't". If you just get out and see customers and pull your products out of the bag, you are bound to sell something.

Figure out ways to see more customers and your sales can't help but increase. Plan your days better, cut down on drive time, and don't procastinate. Stretch every minute of the day all with the intent of seeing more customers.

36 RESPOND IMMEDIATELY TO YOUR CUSTOMERS

First, you should be checking voice mail, at least once in the morning, at noon, in the afternoon, and right before you retire for the evening. When you get a message from a customer, you should immediately respond to them. One of the things customers feel "great reps" do on a consistent basis is that they respond quickly to their needs and their phone calls.

Not only is it your job to sell customers your products, but it is also your responsibility to keep them happy, by providing good follow-up service so that they continue to use your products. If you don't, there are several other reps, waiting right behind you in line, who are willing to get the job done and take your business and your customers.

American Airlines did a study in the mid-90's and found that for every person who complains, there are 24 other unhappy customers who don't say anything. Of that group that doesn't complain, 75% to 90% will never be a customer of that company again. Of those who do complain, 82% to 95% will come back if their problem is addressed promptly.

37 | SELL YOUR PRODUCTS TO EVERYONE

Let me emphasize this importmant point. To be a top rep, you must make sure that you identify who the key decision makers are in your market and focus on those people. But in some industries, there is a lot of down time, so you could be using that time to sell to anyone and everyone who could have any type of influence on the purchase of your product. I'm talking about secondary or even tertiary level people. While they may not be the key decision makers they can definitely have an influence on those key decision makers. So, never ignore anyone. If you believe in your product, you should sell it to everyone you meet. I go to parties and when people ask about my products, I give them the whole "scoop". I can't tell you how many people have told me that they went to their physicians, asked about those products, and next thing you know, their doctor used it on them.

Sure, by targeting and focusing, you will identify the key decision maker but by the same token, don't ignore anyone. Many medical sales trainers or managers will tell the new reps that calling on the surgeons or key physicians is where they should spend their time. If you have a physician driven product, then I agree you should spend "most" of your time with them, but you should not ignore the other people who have an influence on the purchase of your product. This includes nurses, scrub techs, physician assistants, OR Material Coordinators, OR Managers, and even material managers, when necessary. This holds true for any industry.

If you sell other products in other industries, be sure not to exclude people that could have an influence on the decision making process as well. Many sales books you may read emphasize that you should quickly identify who the decision maker is and not waste time with other people. I agree to a large extent, but I just don't think you should ignore anyone. I know exactly what some sales trainers are talking about when they say you should not waste time with people that aren't the decision makers. There are products, such as homes, cars, or other similar products that you may be wasting your time trying to sell their 18 year old son, or one spouse over the other, on your product.

I can't tell you how many times I have gone in to look at a house or vacation home, and the sales people really push for me to bring my wife before they really spend a lot of intense time with me. Why? Because their experience tells them that one spouse alone rarely makes a decision on a home without the other. So, in this regard, they are using their time wisely. They are working smart which is wise. But, when you have down time, sell to everyone. If you are in a model home, and only three or four prospects come a day, why not spend time with one spouse; get them excited, then hopefully they will come back. If people are busting down your doors, lined up to talk about your homes, then I can understand you weeding out based on the percentages.

You just need to determine if those rules apply to your business, and then use them as guidelines. It seems as though most products touch the hands of many people and thus you should be careful ignoring anyone. You must be very careful about this approach of bypassing people, because it can often come back to haunt you. If you are selling copiers, the main decision maker may be the office manager, but while the product is in the office on evaluation, who is going to be using it the majority of the time, the office manager or the secretary? I just believe you must cover all your bases and insure you sell your product to everyone.

All too many times, sales reps exclude these other people who end up being roadblocks to your success. For instance, if you ignore a surgical tech, never in-service them, or give them the time of day, they may find it offensive. They are standing next to that surgeon almost every day, at the operating room table. You will be making a big mistake by ignoring them. If they decide they don't like you and they like your competitor better, the scrub tech is going to be selling against you every day. They will plant little seeds of doubt and might even "flat out" tell the doctor they think you are a "snake" and tell them no one likes you. Obviously, this could be the "kiss of death" and you may never know it happened, except for the fact that you never got the business.

38 | WHAT SHOULD YOU DO FIRST IN YOUR TERRITORY?

"The ability to concentrate and to use your time well is everything."

LEE IACOCCA

After a number of years managing sales reps, a former colleague of mine went to work for another company as a rep himself. He gave me a call and asked me what I thought he should do first. This is what I told him:

i. Immediately identify your top current accounts; those with the largest dollar volume in sales. Ask the company for the prior sales reports for at least the last six months to a year and hopefully for the last few years as well. Sort these accounts based on existing dollar volume with the largest accounts first. During training, call the accounts, and let them know you are the new rep and you will be out to see them in a few weeks, after you finish training. You might even encourage your manager to get in and see the largest accounts, just to be sure they are feeling loved.

ii. Go visit and see those accounts the day you step foot in the territory and begin fostering relationships to "build a fence around your existing business". Throw a happy hour, dinner, do an in-service or go on a golf outing, but do whatever it takes to become friends with your customers. The competitors have been waiting in line to take that business and because you are new, the business is vulnerable. The accounts had loyalty to your predecessor, but not necessarily to you or the company.

iii. Do not wait to be an expert on your products. Do not pro-crastinate. Trying to become an expert is a form of procrastination. Explain to the customers that you are new and learning and they will usually go out of their way to teach you and help you. Don't sit in your office trying to be an expert. If you were busting your rear end in training, you should have the basis of knowledge to prevent you from looking totally incompetent.

iv. Pull your products out of the bag and begin selling. You don't have to be overly aggressive. Just don't wait six months to start selling. Sell immediately. If you don't know the answer to a question, let the customer know you'll get back to them. Once you have the answer, you'll never forget it. Tell the customer, "Hey, we just released this product and it seems to be doing extremely well. As one of my largest customers I wanted to get your opinion and I wanted to avoid you being mad at me for not showing it to you for six months. Then begin asking questions and you just might find yourself making a sale.

v. Work to have an immediate impact as you promised the hiring manager when you interviewed for the job.

vi. Get to know the most successful reps. Find out who they are and give them a call. Ask them their views and tactics. You will become fast friends, as you are paying them the highest sales compliment. They will go out of their way to help you.

vii. Set your written goals and specific targets. Have an action plan for the first 30, 60 and 90 days. Update it at least weekly.

Here is a great checklist for any sales rep beginning a new job, or even a tenured rep that may need to review the basics. If you can truly put a check next to each of these items, you will be on your way to Top Success!

CHECKLIST FOR SUCCESS

PREPARATION:

A. PRODUCT KNOWLEDGE
- Be an expert with your products.(Within 6 months)
- Be an expert with your competitor's products. (Within 6 months)
- Be an expert with your clinical or technical papers as well as your competitor's. (Within 6 months)
- Utilize ongoing information, provided by your company or industry magazines, bulletins, meetings, training, etc.
- Find or develop new product applications with the help of your teammates or customers.
- Develop effective sales presentations.

B. ACCOUNT KNOWLEDGE
- Know your customer.
- Review the former reps account files and sales reports.
- Speak to others within the company that may know the customers well.
- Speak to distributors, dealers, or other non-competitive reps that may know the customer.

C. DEVELOP CALL OBJECTIVES (All calls are sales calls)
- Have written, specific overall goals.
- Break them down to monthly, weekly, and daily goals.
- Have a daily written work plan.
- Have specific sales objectives on all calls.
- Find out who the key decision makers are, and be sure to focus on them.
- Don't procrastinate and waste time. Eliminate time wasters.
- Sell the profitable or emphasis products that your company wants you to sell, not what is easiest.
- Sell the "whole bag" of products.

- Follow-up with customers with thank you notes, letters, clinical papers or anything else to support your products and your relationships.

D. DEVELOP EFFECTIVE CALL PATTERNS AND ROUTING
- Minimize "wind-shield" time or lost travel time.
- Make appointments versus "just dropping in".
- Send reminders or leave a message reminding customers of your appointment.
- Call on LARGE ACCOUNTS under competitive threat, every week until you have squashed the attack. If you want to win the war, you've got to fight the battles.
- Call on NEWLY CONVERTED ACCOUNTS, especially those that have big complainers, also once per week; minimum.
- Call on your Top 10-15 accounts at least once every 2 weeks.
- Your next 16-25 accounts should be called upon every 3-4 weeks.
- Large, STONE WALLED ACCOUNTS should be called on at least every 4-8 weeks. If you want to continue growing your business and developing new accounts, it is important you don't ignore any large account. A stone walled account is one that you are having a hard time penetrating, as if it were surrounded by a stone wall. If you keep hitting the stone wall, eventually you will break through.

E. CALL PREPARATION
- Be fully prepared.
- Prepare specific materials for each call to be presented.
- Keep your brochures and demo equipment in good presentable condition.
- Practice your presentations so that you are confident and knowledgeable.
- Make sure your detail bag and trunk stock are well stocked and ready for every situation.

After you have prepared yourself, learned all the material, developed your call objectives, and you are now in the call, every great sales rep follows a process that will lead to the most important point of a sales call?..........................that's right, closing the sales and getting the order for your product!!!!!

I have taken many selling courses, each with their own acronym for the "Steps of the Sale" but they are all basically the same. An excellent book on this subject is Ron Willingham's "Integrity Selling", which I highly recommend.

The steps of the sales are very straightforward, and if you fail to follow these steps, you will often find yourself empty- handed. Basically, they are:

Introduce yourself to the customer or if you already know them, open the conversation, briefly, with social, small talk, and show a sincere interest and concern for them and their business.

1) Give the customer an **outline** of what you would like to cover.

2) **Ask** the customer **open ended questions** to determine their needs and then zero in on specific areas.
Repeat back to your customer, what you believe you heard them state as their needs. This shows that you were listening and that you care.

3) **Demonstrate** your product, which fits those needs, all the while, continuing to ask questions, which **lead** the customer to believe and understand that your product meets those needs.

4) Be sure to **bring the customer into the demonstration**. Let them hold the product. Allow them to comment and be interactive during the demonstration.

5) Ask questions to **determine** any **concerns**.

6) Next, **close the sale** and ask for the business, or at a minimum, ask for action to be taken by the customer, which will lead to a sale.

7) Don't forget to **follow-up** and insure that they continue to use your product. Insure that you answer any questions but don't oversell. Most of the time, the person who bought the product, is not the only one who will use the product. You will need to insure that you:

8) **In-service all personnel** that will use your product, otherwise, the whole process could be sabotaged or fail.

39 | SUMMARY

Keep in mind, that in order to be successful and a top sales rep, you don't have to possess all of the traits or mindsets I've described in this book. Although, the more of them you work to improve or obtain, through your selling career, the better you will become. If you have the burning desire and obsession to succeed, you will work hard to grow and become better. Top sales reps are always working to better themselves, to get one leg up on their competition. So if you don't currently possess all of these traits, don't feel as though you can't ever become a sales rep. These are mental commitments that you can demand of yourself to happen quickly, if you are disciplined.

If you demand of yourself that you will always be totally honest with your customers, then why can't you just be totally honest with your customers? Done. If you demand that you will take total responsibility for your results, then do it! Accomplished! It's interesting to note, that most traits of a top sales rep are just that, a state of mind, an attitude. You don't have to be a "smooth operator". You don't have to be the funniest guy or gal around. You don't have to be filled with "tricky" questions.

Probably, the hardest challenge for many is the fear of rejection but you and most people can definitely overcome this fear. In fact, overcoming your fear of rejection in sales can lead to other benefits in your personal life as well. The more you put yourself in uncomfortable situations; the more you get out there and start "detailing" your product, the better you are going to get. You will eventually obtain so much confidence in your presentations and in yourself that you can be put in almost any situation and you will shine. You'll begin to realize that the more quality sales calls and presentations you make, the more business you will close, and the more you will be able to tolerate the rejection when someone doesn't buy from you.

So remember, set the written goal to be a top sales rep or to be the best at whatever you do. Back that goal with a burning desire and you will reach the top at whatever you do. You will overcome all your fears, and you will become the best of the best!

I wish you all the success at everything you try. I hope you are given the strength and fortitude to work hard and stay with it until you succeed. It's much better to be the best at what you do as opposed to being average. Once you walk up on stage for the first time, it will drive you crazy to sit in the audience the next year and not win an award. It is definitely contagious but you've got to get up there the first time to catch the spirit.

I wish you the GREATEST success and the GREATEST life.

Please go to www.deangould.com and download free worksheets on goal setting, account targeting, rolling 30, 60, 90 opportunity sheets, and strength/weakness analysis.

For medical and pharmaceutical sales representatives, you will also find a free addendum on how to excel calling on physicians.

You will also find additional free information, downloads, and material that will help enhance your selling career and personal development.

SUGGESTED ADDITIONAL READING:

Think and Grow Rich
Napoleon Hill

Success Through a Positive Mental Attitude
Napoleon Hill & W. Clement Stone

How to Win Friends and Influence People
Dale Carnegie

The Richest Man in Babylon
George S. Clason

The Greatest Salesman in the World
Og Mandino

Swim with the Sharks Without Being Eaten Alive
Harvey Mackay

How to Master the Art of Selling Anything
Tom Hopkins

Integrity Selling
Bob Willingham

See You at the Top
Zig Zigler

Rhinoceros Success
Scott Alexader